In Heaven itself, I'll ask no more,
than just a Highland welcome.

— **Robert Burns**

# I LOVE FOOD

2

Clare Russell is Lady Laird of the romantic Ballindalloch Castle, in Banffshire.

Following on from the remarkable success of her last cookery book, "I Love Food", Clare now presents a simply elegant second helping of recipes reflecting her love of food, family and the ravishing Speyside surroundings she adores.

## A SMILE

A smile costs nothing, but gives much. It enriches those who receive, without making poorer those who give. It takes but a moment, but the memory of it sometimes lasts forever. None is so rich or mighty that he can get along without it, and none is so poor but that he can be made rich by it. A smile creates happiness in the home, fosters goodwill in business, and is the countersign of friendship. It brings rest to the weary, cheer to the discouraged, sunshine to the sad, and it is nature's best antidote for trouble. Yet it cannot be bought, begged, borrowed or stolen, for it is something that is of no value to anyone until it is given away.

Some people are too tired to give you a smile, give them one of yours, as none needs a smile so much as he who has no more to give.

*Clare Russell*

From "Bumble"
to my beloved grandchildren

**Iona, Bertie, George, Louisa, Flora, Rose & Cara**

Live well,
Laugh often,
Love much.

THE UNIQUE BEST-SELLING COOKBOOK

## "I LOVE FOOD"

CLARE MACPHERSON-GRANT RUSS...

# "I LOVE FOOD 2"

## An introduction by Clare Macpherson-Grant Russell

I never thought that I would write another cookbook but, having received many very kind e-mails asking for a further taste, here I go again with second helpings in 'I Love Food 2'. Those who enjoyed the first book will already know the history of how it all began but new readers may like to know a little about my background.

My parents were fortunate enough to inherit Ballindalloch Castle from a cousin in 1950 when I was five years old. It had been the family home of the Macpherson-Grants since they built it in 1546. As I was the only member of the family left it was made clear to me from an early age that it would be my duty to keep the historic property alive - a tall order at that time as it was a typically dark and dank castle and was on its last legs. There was no proper central heating, only basic electricity with lights that fizzed every time you switched them on, one bathroom in the whole castle, and when it rained we had to lay out endless buckets! My parents had to make a major decision; whether to renovate or to leave Ballindalloch to become yet another ruin. Luckily, they had the great foresight to gut the building and renovate it from top to toe, a process that took over three years.

I had the most wonderful childhood at Ballindalloch. As an only child I was brought up by a governess, whom I loved dearly, and who taught me everything I know. I think she would be smiling down at me now as I had the great honour last year of being awarded an Honorary Degree from the University of Aberdeen. When my father died I became the first Lady Laird of Ballindalloch and the 22nd generation of my family to live here. I was very lucky to have met my husband, Oliver, who was prepared to marry me, my castle and my dogs, and move to Scotland!

We returned to Banffshire to take over the castle from my parents in 1978. It was then that my great love of food and cooking began. Taking one look at the estate accounts my husband, a banker, decided that the castle and estate had to be commercialised and become a serious business if they were to survive. We had enough money to pay one member of staff, but we had 30. This concentrated the mind a little, and I had to become chief cook and bottle washer at breakneck speed! The first thing I had to do was learn to cook. As I had never had a cookery lesson in my life Oliver kindly suggested I should go to Elgin Library and consult some recipe books. I thumbed through at least 50 and chose the easiest recipes with the least number of ingredients, telling myself 'surely, if you can read, you can cook'! Although how I had the confidence to cook for some of the most sophisticated of corporate parties I will never know ...

'I Love Food' was derived from many recipes, concocted over the years. It has been a surprising success and it is still selling after 8 years and 15 reprints. I adore food but I am not prepared to spend hours slaving over a cooker, so my motto is still very definitely 'taste, ease and speed'. We have had enormous fun putting 'I Love Food 2' together. All the recipes are well tested by Kenny Flesh, and the fantastic food images were styled by him and John Paul, who took the stunning photographs. Their talent and expertise is exceptional. All the photographs were taken inside or round about the Castle, using china, textiles and various objects which are part of our family history. I have had much enthusiastic help too, from my husband, children and grandchildren, to dogs, cats, birds and the red squirrels resident in the grounds and estate.

I do not in any way presume to be a 'Masterchef' - just a home cook who loves traditional food. I have two recipe categories: 'posh food' and 'comfort food', and in this book I hope that I have shown you that even easy recipes can be made to be 'simply elegant'.

I have also included a collection of favourite poems, quotations and quirky fun bits! My beloved dogs are, of course, included and this time, as well as 'Woof' I have added 'Miaow' and 'Tweet'! I received a lovely e-mail from an Australian cat requesting that, in my next book, I have a section for felines. As a result I have spent two days trying out 'moggie munchies', 'cat cupcakes' and 'rabbit ragout'. I never want to smell another sardine or pilchard! 'Tweet' is for twitchers and bird-lovers and is a bit of fun in this 21st century 'Twitter' era. As well as for garden birds, I have also included a selection of nuts for red squirrels, which are fast becoming extinct in large parts of the UK. We are lucky enough here to have a good number of them and we do everything to try to ensure their survival.

You might think, if you watch television, that everyone aspires to cooking like a celebrity chef, but in reality few of us have the time. I hope that 'I Love Food 2' bridges this gap. I am indebted to those people who have helped, offered advice, tweaked recipes, tasted and criticised. Top of the list are my wonderful husband and family who give me confidence and support - my most grateful thanks to you all.

This book would never have come to fruition without the skills and enthusiasm of: my chef, Kenny Flesh; John Paul, who has produced the most stunning photographs; our Factor, Tim Atkinson; our Estate Secretary, Kath Davies; Production Assistant, Karen Flesh; my Personal Assistant, Fenella Corr; and all the team at Ballindalloch. Also a big thank you to Jamieson Eley at Hudson's Media. I do hope that you will enjoy reading this book as much as I have enjoyed writing it, and that your motto, too, will become 'simply elegant'.

**Happy cooking.**

Clare Macpherson-Grant Russell.

# WHEN YOU ARE LONELY

*When you are lonely, I wish you love*
*When you are down, I wish you joy*
*When you are troubled, I wish you simply beauty*
*When things are chaotic, I wish you inner silence*
*When things look empty, I wish you hope*
*I wish for both of you, a giant book imprinted on your souls*
*Where you shall keep all the memories you will make together*
*I wish for a group of angels hovering over both of you*
*Every second, every minute of your lives*
*I wish for both of you, happiness and the faith to see*
*That God blessed you both when He gave you to each other*

*Anonymous*

"taste, ease and speed"

*Clare Russell*

The Dining Room
at Ballindalloch

# CASTLE Cooking

# Starting Out

Asparagus wrapped in Parma Ham
with a Herby Hollandaise .......................... 16

Avocado Terrine ........................................ 18

Charentais Melon, Parma Ham
& Buffalo Mozzarella ................................ 20

Pan-roasted King Scallops served
on a pool of Green Pea & Mint Purée
sprinkled with Crispy Pancetta ............. 22

Timbales of Portsoy Crab
with an Avocado Sauce ............................ 24

Pea Timbales served with
Mint Hollandaise ...................................... 26

Smoked Salmon Castles filled with
Avocado Mousse ...................................... 28

Smoked Salmon, Cucumber
& Egg Mousse .......................................... 30

Smoked Salmon &
Quail's Egg Tartlets ................................. 34

Ballindalloch Seafood Cocktail .............. 36

Twice-baked Goat's Cheese
Soufflés with a Cream & Leek Sauce .. 38

Smoked Haddock &
Avocado Creams ...................................... 40

Spey Salmon &
Lemon Mascarpone Terrine ..................... 44

Crab Tartlets ............................................. 46

Warm Avocados with
Scallops & Bacon ..................................... 46

Parma Ham, Goat's Cheese &
Figs on a bed of Rocket sprinkled
with Parmesan .......................................... 47

Mushroom & Stilton Twirls ...................... 47

Tomato, Pepper & Orange Soup ........... 49

Butternut Squash Soup with a
touch of Coconut ..................................... 49

Carrot & Orange Soup ............................. 50

Celeriac & Celery Soup ........................... 50

Mint Pea Soup sprinkled with
Streaky Bacon .......................................... 51

Parsnip & Apple Soup .............................. 51

Mushroom with Stilton Soup ................... 52

# ASPARAGUS wrapped in PARMA HAM with a HERBY Hollandaise

(serves 6)

## INGREDIENTS
24 asparagus spears
12 slices of Parma ham,
halved widthways
2 tablespoons extra virgin olive oil
Juice of ½ a lemon

### For Herby Hollandaise:
4 egg yolks
1 tablespoon water
2 tablespoons lemon juice
1 tablespoon finely chopped herbs
(buy fresh mixture)
6fl oz (150g) melted butter
Salt and pepper

## METHOD
Wrap each asparagus spear in half a
slice of ham and place on baking sheet.
Drizzle with 2 tablespoons oil and lemon
juice. Roast in oven for 10 minutes at
350°F/180°C/Gas 4 until cooked and
ham is crispy. Meanwhile, make Herby
Hollandaise. Whisk egg yolks, water and
lemon juice in bowl over a pan of simmering
water. Pour in hot melted butter and whisk
until thick. Season and add chopped herbs.
Drizzle sauce over top of asparagus.

*What could
be better
on a spring
evening?*

'Spring is when life's alive in everything.'

# AVOCADO Terrine

(serves 6)

## INGREDIENTS
2 avocados + 1 avocado for centre
4 leaves of gelatine
½ pint (300ml) of mayonnaise
1 wine glass of dry white wine
Squeeze of lemon juice
Bag of rocket for serving
Dash of Worcestershire sauce
Salt and pepper

Dear Lady Macpherson-Grant Russel
I would just like to tell you that I am
working my way through your wonderful
"I LOVE FOOD" Cookbook. I am a Housekeeper
to a gentleman who entertains a lot. I am
so pleased that he and his guests so enjoy the food thanks to your recipes, which
are so easy to follow. My cooking skills
have improved enormously as has my confidence in trying the recipes out. May I
wish you and your family a HAPPY CHRIST
MAS, and thank you again.

Pam Thomas

P.S. I have visited your beautiful Castle
many years ago and treasure the memory.

## METHOD
Place 4 gelatine leaves in a bowl and cover with
water to soften. Pour the wine into a pan and
warm over a gentle heat. Remove the gelatine
from the water, squeeze to remove excess water
then dissolve it in the wine. Leave to cool, then
whisk in mayonnaise. Peel, halve and stone 2
avocados. Liquidise. Add to the mixture. Season
and add a dash of Worcestershire sauce. Line
a 1 pint (600ml) loaf tin with cling film allowing
it to hang over the edges. Pour half avocado
mixture into the bottom of the tin and leave to
set. Peel, halve and stone remaining avocado.
Place along the length of the tin and pour over
the remaining avocado mixture. Leave to set for
several hours. To serve, turn onto plate and slice.
Serve individually accompanied with rocket salad
drizzled with French dressing and walnut bread.

Simple and pretty.

# Charentais MELON, PARMA HAM & Buffalo MOZZARELLA

(serves 4)

## INGREDIENTS
8 slices Parma ham
1 charentais melon,
peeled and sliced thinly
2 buffalo Mozzarella,
approximately 8oz (225g)
Mint leaves for decoration
Balsamic dressing

## METHOD
Fan out a quarter of sliced melon on each plate, place some sliced Mozzarella by its side, and the Parma ham is scrunched or rolled. Drizzle balsamic dressing across the plate. Scatter with mint leaves.

*A good one
for perfecting
your own style.*

*A delightful summer dish.*

# Pan-roasted KING SCALLOPS served on a pool of GREEN PEA & MINT Purée sprinkled with Crispy PANCETTA

(serves 4)

## INGREDIENTS
12 king scallops
Clarified butter for pan frying
8 slices pancetta or streaky bacon
(grilled until crispy)
14oz (400g) frozen peas
½oz (15g) mint leaves
2oz (50ml) double cream (optional)
Salt and freshly ground black pepper

## METHOD
Cook the peas in salted boiling water for about 4–6 minutes or until tender. Drain. Blend peas with mint (or, alternatively, marjoram leaves would be nice). If mixture is too thick to blend easily, add a few drops of cream. Season to taste with salt and pepper, then return to saucepan. Re-heat gently for serving. Pan-fry scallops in butter for 1–2 minutes each side, depending on size, and serve on a pool of pea and mint purée, sprinkled with pancetta or crisped streaky bacon.

*The first starter recipe I would take to my desert island.*

# Timbales of Portsoy CRAB with an AVOCADO Sauce

(serves 4)

## INGREDIENTS
8oz (225g) good white crab meat
3fl oz (90ml) natural yogurt plus 2 extra tablespoons for avocado sauce
1oz (25g) fresh coriander, chopped
Juice of 1 lemon
2 avocados
Dash of Worcestershire sauce
4 tomatoes (sliced for decoration)
Salt and pepper

## METHOD
Check through crab and remove any shell, then add yogurt, chopped coriander and lemon juice. Mix well and season to taste. Place crab mixture into rings in centre of plate. Leave to chill for 2 hours. Meanwhile halve, stone and skin avocados. Place in liquidiser with 2 tablespoons of yogurt and a dash of Worcestershire sauce. Season. Remove rings from crab, serve with avocado sauce and decorate with sliced tomatoes.

*The Portsoy Boat Festival is held each year to celebrate the community's relationship with, and historical dependence on the sea.*
Photo: Kathy Mansfield

*Another recipe I would definitely take to a desert island.*

# PEA Timbales served with MINT Hollandaise

(serves 4-6)

## INGREDIENTS

2lbs (800g) fresh or frozen peas
12oz (300g) soured cream
4 eggs and 1 extra egg yolk
2 tablespoons parmesan cheese

### For mint hollandaise:

4 egg yolks
1 tablespoon water
2 tablespoons lemon juice
1 tablespoon finely chopped mint
6oz (150g) melted butter
Salt and pepper

## Clare's tip:

*If the Hollandaise curdles, throw
in an ice cube and beat like mad!*

## METHOD

Cook peas in boiling water until
tender. Drain and liquidise until
smooth. Sieve. Whisk eggs in
bowl and fold in cream and
Parmesan cheese. Stir in pea
purée. Pour mixture into six
lightly buttered timbale moulds.
Cover each mould with piece of
greased foil. Place in a bain-marie
(roasting tin half-filled with hot
water). Bake at 350°F/180°C/
Gas 4 for about 25–30 minutes
until set. Remove moulds from
bain-marie and let stand for a
few minutes before turning onto
serving plates. Serve surrounded
by warm mint Hollandaise.

### For mint hollandaise:

Whisk egg yolks, water and lemon
juice in bowl over hot water. Pour
in hot melted butter and whisk
until thick. Season and add finely
chopped mint.

*A starter to rave about.*

# SMOKED SALMON Castles
# filled with AVOCADO Mousse

**(serves 6-8)**

## INGREDIENTS
8oz (225g) sliced smoked salmon
3 ripe avocados
(skinned, halved and stoned)
½lb (225g) cream cheese
Few drops Tabasco and
Worcestershire sauce
Juice of ½ lemon
2 lemons
Parsley for decoration
Salt and pepper

## METHOD
Rinse out small ramekins with cold water and line with smoked salmon slices, overlapping edges. Purée avocados, cream cheese, sauces, juice of ½ lemon and salt and pepper together. Divide mixture between ramekins and cover with overlapping salmon. Cover with tin foil and place in fridge for several hours to set. Turn out and garnish with lemons and parsley or, if time permits garnish with avocados and quail's eggs surrounded with lemon, pepper and chive dressing. Serve with home-made brown bread and butter.

*A delicious, easy and colourful first course.*

"Obair-na-Ghaol" from Portsoy joins The Queen's Diamond Jubilee Pageant on the river Thames.

# SMOKED SALMON, CUCUMBER & EGG Mousse

(serves 6-8)

## INGREDIENTS
8oz (225g) smoked salmon
3 large hard boiled eggs
3 tablespoons Greek yoghurt or
crème fraîche
½oz (12g) gelatine
1 teaspoon anchovy essence
7fl oz (180ml) white sauce, cooled
½ cucumber finely diced
3 tablespoons fresh chopped
parsley/dill
Lemon or lime juice to taste
¼pt (150ml) whipping cream
3 tablespoons dry vermouth,
or water
Bag of rocket
Salt and pepper

## METHOD
Lightly brush six individual moulds with melted butter. Pour vermouth, or water, into pan and sprinkle over gelatine. Set aside for 5–10 minutes. Meanwhile peel and chop hard boiled eggs, then finely chop smoked salmon. Mix Greek yoghurt, or crème fraîche, anchovy essence, chopped boiled eggs, diced cucumber and smoked salmon with white sauce. Season and add a few drops of lemon or lime juice. Melt gelatine over a gentle heat without boiling until clear.

Stir into smoked salmon mixture, then fold in lightly whipped cream. Spoon into moulds. Chill overnight. To serve slip a hot knife around the edge of mousse and invert onto serving plate surrounded with rocket. Accompany with melba toast.

*Can be done the night before a dinner party, so really useful.*

A Spey 'monster' of 38lbs

THE ANGLER'S PRAYER

Lord give me grace
to catch a fish
So large that even I,
when talking of it
afterwards,
May never need to lie.

# SMOKED SALMON
# & QUAIL'S EGG Tartlets

**(serves 4)**

## INGREDIENTS
4 savoury tartlet cases
(make or buy)
12 quail's eggs
4oz (100g) sliced smoked salmon

### For hollandaise:
4 egg yolks
1 tablespoon water
2 tablespoons lemon juice
6oz (150g) melted butter
A little dill for decoration
Salt and pepper

## METHOD
Place tartlets in oven to warm.
Meanwhile, make Hollandaise: whisk
egg yolks, water and lemon juice in
bowl over hot water. Pour in melted
butter in steady stream and whisk
until thick. Season. Keep warm. Poach
quail's eggs in hot water with a little
vinegar for about 1–1½ minutes. When
cooked, but still soft, take out with
slotted spoon and place on kitchen
paper until dry. Place smoked salmon
in tartlets, with eggs in middle, and
pour Hollandaise over the top. Sprinkle
with dill. Serve immediately.

*Easy, tasty and speedy.*

### Clare's tip:
*If the Hollandaise curdles, throw
in an ice cube and beat like mad!*

# Ballindalloch SEAFOOD Cocktail

(serves 6-8)

## INGREDIENTS
1 iceberg lettuce, finely shredded
9oz (250g) king prawns
cooked and peeled
(keep 6 large prawns for decoration)
Crab (1 shell)
Lobster pieces (if possible)
Lime wedges to serve
Cayenne pepper to finish
12 quail's eggs, lightly boiled in shell for 3 minutes
Seafood sauce (buy 2 bottles)

## METHOD
Make a bed of lettuce at bottom of 6 glasses. Mix prawns, crab, lobster and halved quail's eggs together with seafood sauce and spoon on top of lettuce. Sprinkle with cayenne pepper, add a wedge of lime and top with a prawn. Serve with brown bread and butter.

*An old-fashioned recipe with a new twist!*

# Twice–baked GOAT'S CHEESE Soufflés with a CREAM & LEEK Sauce

**(Serves 6)**

## INGREDIENTS
6oz (150g) goat's cheese
½pt (300ml) milk
2oz (50g) butter
2oz (50g) flour
Pinch of dried mustard
4 eggs plus 1 extra egg white
½pt (300ml) double cream
6 tablespoons grated Parmesan
1 leek, finely sliced and blanched in boiling water
Salt and pepper

## METHOD
Melt butter, flour, mustard and milk slowly together, whisking like mad until it comes to boil. Add the goat's cheese and salt and pepper. Separate eggs and add egg yolks to sauce. Whisk all whites and fold into cheese mixture. Spoon into buttered ramekins, filling almost to the top. Stand in bain-marie (a baking tin half-filled with hot water) and bake for 15 minutes at 350°F/180°C/Gas 4. Cool and leave in ramekins.

Twenty minutes before dinner, run a knife round the soufflés to loosen and turn out onto individual ear dishes. Mix finely chopped and blanched leek with cream. Season and pour over each soufflé. Sprinkle with Parmesan and bake at 350°F/180°C/Gas 4 for 10 minutes. Serve immediately.

*My husband Oliver's Russell family coat of arms, features a goat above the motto: 'che sara sara' - what will be, will be.*

*A reliable life-saver that never fails and can be made in the morning or the day before.*

# SMOKED HADDOCK
# & AVOCADO creams

(serves 4)

## INGREDIENTS
½lb (225g) smoked haddock
2 avocados (peeled,
halved and stoned)
1oz (25g) butter
1oz (25g) plain flour
½pt (300ml) single cream
3oz (75g) grated cheddar cheese
Salt and pepper

*A real discovery -
good easy starter
and also a great
supper dish.*

## METHOD
Simmer smoked haddock in cream
until cooked. Strain and reserve liquid.
Melt butter in saucepan, add flour
and cook for one minute. Gradually
add reserved liquid, whisking like
mad to prevent lumps. Simmer for
1–2 minutes. Fold in flaked fish and
season. Spoon into ramekins, top with
a sliced, fanned out half avocado,
sprinkle liberally with grated cheese
and grill until cheese is melted and
bubbling or bake for 8–10 minutes at
400°F/200°C/Gas 6.

*SCOTTISH ANGLER'S LAMENT*

*Sometimes ower early,*
*sometimes ower late,*
*Sometimes nae water,*
*sometimes a spate,*
*Sometimes ower dirty,*
*sometimes ower clear,*
*There's aye something wrang,*
*when I'm fishin' here.*

Junction Pool on
River Spey at Ballindalloch

# Spey SALMON & LEMON MASCARPONE Terrine
(serves 6-8)

## INGREDIENTS

8oz (200g) sliced smoked salmon (line 2lb loaf tin with cling film then line with sliced smoked salmon)

### For mascarpone mousse:
1 egg yolk
3oz (75g) mascarpone cheese
1 gelatine leaf
Horseradish sauce
3fl oz (75ml) double cream
Salt and pepper
Lemon juice
Rind of ½ lemon

### For salmon mousse:
½lb (200g) cooked salmon
2 tablespoons fish stock
¼pt (150ml) cream
2oz (50ml) mayonnaise
1oz (25g) softened butter
2fl oz (60ml) sherry
1 tablespoon lemon juice
4 leaves gelatine (soaked)
6oz (175g) cucumber, diced
Smoked salmon trimmings, chopped
1oz (25g) mixed herbs, chopped
Tabasco, mustard & seasoning

## METHOD

### For mascarpone mousse:
Soak gelatine leaf in some cold water. Whisk egg yolk with mascarpone cheese. Heat a little lemon juice and dissolve the gelatine in it, then mix into the cheese mixture. Lightly whip cream and fold in. Season, add lemon rind and horseradish sauce. Pour into the terrine, level mousse and place in fridge.

### For salmon mousse:
Soak gelatine leaves in cold water. Meanwhile, place the cooked salmon into food processor with cream, mayonnaise, softened butter, sherry and lemon juice and liquidise until smooth. Drain soaked gelatine leaves and squeeze to remove excess water. Add to the warmed fish stock, cool and add to the mousse. Season with salt, pepper, Tabasco and mustard. Whizz. Remove from liquidiser and spoon into bowl. Add chopped smoked salmon, diced cucumber and chopped herbs. Pour onto mascarpone mousse and level off. Overlap smoked salmon neatly. Chill until set. To serve, dip into hot water briefly, then unmould onto serving platter. Garnish with cooked prawns and asparagus spears.

*A big favourite.*

# CRAB Tartlets

**(serves 6)**

*I think I must have been a fisherman in my past life, as I adore seafood!*

## INGREDIENTS
12oz (350g) ready-rolled shortcrust pastry (or use ready-made tartlet cases)
10oz (275g) good crabmeat
1 tablespoon freshly grated Parmesan cheese
1 egg and 1 egg yolk
¼pt (150ml) double cream
1 tablespoon fresh chopped parsley
Salt and pepper
Pinch cayenne pepper

## METHOD
Roll out pastry thinly on floured surface. Cut into 6 squares and line 6 x 4" (10cm) round fluted loose-bottomed greased tins. Bake blind in oven for 8–10 minutes at 400°F/200°C/Gas 6. Cool. Reduce heat to 350°F/180°C/Gas 4. Meanwhile, whisk egg and egg yolk with cream and pinch of cayenne pepper, lemon juice, parsley and season. Place pastry cases on baking tray and divide crabmeat between each one. Pour over egg mixture to ¾ fill the cases. Sprinkle each with Parmesan. Bake for 15–20 minutes until firm to touch. Serve with rocket salad.

# Warm AVOCADOS with SCALLOPS and BACON

**(serves 4)**

*I love scallops, although they can be difficult to source fresh.*

## INGREDIENTS
2 avocados, halved and stoned
8 slices of streaky bacon
4 tablespoons Hellman's mayonnaise
4oz (100g) prawns
4 tablespoons of grated Cheddar cheese
2 tablespoons of good oil
12 queen scallops

## METHOD
Fry bacon and chop. Scoop flesh out of avocado and dice. Mix diced avocado and prawns into mayonnaise. Place in ear dishes or large ramekins. Heat oil and sauté trimmed queen scallops for about 2 minutes until opaque. Place on top of avocado mixture. Sprinkle with cheese and finely chopped bacon, place in oven 400°F/200°C/Gas 6 for 8 minutes.

# PARMA HAM, GOAT'S CHEESE and FIGS on a bed of ROCKET sprinkled with PARMESAN

(serves 4)

## INGREDIENTS

12 slices of Parma ham
4 ripe figs
Bag of rocket leaves
6oz (150g) soft goat's cheese
Parmesan for sprinkling

### For Dressing:

3 tablespoons olive oil
1 tablespoon white wine vinegar
1 tablespoon runny honey
1 teaspoon fresh thyme
(finely chopped)
Salt and pepper

## METHOD

Mix together all dressing ingredients and season. For the salad, place 3 slices of Parma ham in the middle of 4 plates. Cut the figs into wedges and place with ham. Cut goats' cheese into small pieces and scatter over ham. Top with rocket leaves and sprinkle with dressing. Finish with grated Parmesan. Serve with warm brown bread.

# MUSHROOM & STILTON Twirls

(serves 4)

## INGREDIENTS

4 large open cap mushrooms
(remove and keep stalks)
3 tablespoons olive oil
4oz (100g) Stilton (or blue cheese)
12oz (350g) filo pastry
2oz (50g) butter, melted
Bunch parsley
Bunch rosemary
Salt and pepper

## METHOD

Heat 2 tablespoons of oil in pan. Add mushrooms and cook gently on each side for 5 minutes. Chop parsley, rosemary and mushroom stalks finely in bowl. Season. Cut pastry into 12 squares, each 12" x 12" (30cm x 30cm). Use 3 squares of pastry layered for each twirl. Place mushroom, round side down, on top of each square, spoon mushroom mixture into middle of mushrooms and top with cube of Stilton. Lightly brush edges of pastry squares with melted butter then twist together. Place on lined baking sheet and brush with butter. Bake at 375°F/190°C/Gas 5 for 20 minutes until golden.

# SOUPS

'I live on a good soup,
not on fine words"
Molière

# TOMATO, PEPPER & ORANGE

(serves 4-6)

## INGREDIENTS
14oz (400g) jar roasted
peppers, drained
2 teaspoons golden
caster sugar
1¾pts (1 litre) tomato juice
4 ripe plum tomatoes
½pt (300ml) hot
chicken stock
¾pt (450ml) squeezed
orange juice
Salt and pepper

## METHOD
Place peppers, sugar, half
tomato juice and plum
tomatoes in liquidiser and
whizz until small chunks. Sieve
into pan, stir in stock, orange
juice and remaining tomato
juice. Bring to boil and simmer
for about 10 minutes. Season
with black pepper and serve
with garlic croutons or home-
made bread.

*A different twist on
tomato soup.*

# BUTTERNUT SQUASH
## with a touch of COCONUT

*Given to me by
Margaret Stewart*

(serves 4-6)

## INGREDIENTS
1 butternut squash (peeled)
1 finely chopped onion
1oz (25g) butter
1 teaspoon curry powder
3 tomatoes, de-seeded and chopped
¾pt (450ml) chicken or
vegetable stock
1 tin of Bart spiced coconut milk
Crème fraîche and finely chopped
spring onions for decoration
Salt and pepper

## METHOD
Remove seeds from butternut
squash and cut into small pieces.
Soften finely chopped onion in
melted butter. Stir in curry powder.
Add squash and 3 peeled,
de-seeded and chopped tomatoes.
Stir in stock and salt and pepper.
Bring to boil, cover, and simmer
gently for 20 minutes until squash
is soft. Liquidise and return to pan.
Stir in tin of coconut milk and reheat
gently. Before serving, top with blob
of crème fraîche and sprinkle with
finely chopped spring onions.

# CARROT & ORANGE

(serves 4-6)

## INGREDIENTS
1½lbs (700g) carrots,
peeled and sliced
2 onions (peeled & chopped)
2pts (1.2 litres) chicken stock
Juice and zest of
one medium orange
1oz (25g) butter
Chopped parsley or
chives for decoration
Salt and black pepper

## METHOD
Melt butter and add chopped
onions and carrots. Cook gently
for about 5 minutes. Add stock
(preferably home-made) and
season. Simmer until vegetables
are soft. Cool slightly and purée
in liquidiser. Add juice and zest
of one orange. Reheat gently and
decorate with chopped parsley or
chives.

*Lovely soothing winter soup
and very good for the figure!*

# CELERIAC & CELERY

(serves 4-6)

## INGREDIENTS
1 onion, peeled and
finely chopped
1 tablespoon olive oil
1 celeriac, peeled and
cut into chunks
4 celery stalks, sliced
1 potato, peeled and
cut into chunks
1pt (600ml) vegetable stock
1 bay leaf
Small bunch of chives
½pt (300ml) cream
Finely chopped parsley

## METHOD
Fry onion in olive oil until
transparent, add celeriac, celery
and potato. Cook for a few
minutes. Add vegetable stock and
bay leaf. Bring to boil and then
simmer for 20–30 minutes until
all is soft. Season. Liquidise until
smooth. To serve, add a swirl of
cream at the last moment and
sprinkle with chopped parsley.

# MINT PEA sprinkled with STREAKY BACON

**(Serves 6)**

*An old favourite,
served hot or cold*

## INGREDIENTS
1lb (450g) fresh or frozen peas
½pt (300ml) chicken stock
(preferably home-made)
½pt (300ml) whipping cream
4 rashers of streaky bacon
(fried and finely chopped)
Bunch of mint
Salt and pepper to taste

## METHOD
Bring stock to boil, add peas and
a few mint leaves. Bring back to
boil for 2 minutes. Liquidise, sieve
and season. Chill for 4 hours. Add
cream just before serving and
sprinkle with chopped bacon.
Serve with Mrs. D's walnut bread
see page 206.

# PARSNIP & APPLE

**(serves 4-6)**

## INGREDIENTS
1 dessert apple; cored/peeled/
sliced
1½ lbs (700g) parsnips, peeled,
sliced
1oz (25g) butter
2 pts (1.2 litres) vegetable stock
4 fresh sage leaves
½pt (300ml) single cream
Salt and freshly ground
black pepper
Chopped parsley or grated
Parmesan cheese to garnish

## METHOD
Melt butter in pan, add parsnips
and sliced cooking apple, cook
gently for about 10 minutes,
stirring occasionally. Add stock
and sage. Bring to boil, cover
and simmer for 30 minutes until
parsnips are soft. Remove sage,
then whizz in liquidiser. Return
soup to pan, add cream and
re-heat gently. Season to taste. Top
with sprinkling of chopped parsley
or grated Parmesan cheese.

# MUSHROOM with STILTON

(serves 4-6)

## INGREDIENTS
½lb (225g) fresh
mushrooms plus ¼lb (100g)
for slicing
1oz (25g) butter
1oz (25g) flour
1pt (600ml) good strong
stock (preferably home-
made; stock cubes are
usually inferior in taste and
texture)
½pt (300ml) double cream
2 tablespoons crumbled
Stilton
Salt and pepper

## METHOD
Make sauce with the butter,
flour and stock. Liquidise
mushrooms and add to
sauce. Simmer for 10
minutes. Add cream, sliced
mushrooms, salt and pepper
and crumbled Stilton at the
last minute.

# Useful soup garnishes...

## Some ideas to brighten up and accompany your soups.

1. Cream or crème fraîche swirled into centre before serving
2. Bowls of peeled, de-seeded and finely chopped cucumber.
3. Bowls of peeled, de-seeded and finely chopped tomato.
4. Sprinkling of finely snipped chives, basil, coriander or mint.
5. Sprinkling of grated Cheddar or Parmesan
6. Sprinkling of finely chopped fried streaky bacon.
7. Cheesy French bread - lightly toast thin slices of French bread. Sprinkle with plenty of grated mature cheese and grill until melted and golden - delicious floating on top of soup.
8. Croutons - remove crusts from 4 thick slices of bread and cut into cubes. Heat some vegetable oil in frying pan and, when hot, add cubed bread. Stir fry over medium heat until brown. Remove from pan and drain on kitchen paper.
P.S. Grated cheese or crushed garlic can be added to croutons to give a variety of flavour.
9. Or serve with Mrs D's brown bread, see page 206.

Mad about roulades?
So am I!
They are the epitome of
'taste, ease and speed' –
and failsafe!

# Ravishing Roulades

## Starters:

## Puddings:

# CARROT Roulade with EGG & CRESS filling

**(serves 6)**

*Excellent recipe for vegetarians.*

## INGREDIENTS

### For roulade:
2 level tablespoons freshly-grated Parmesan cheese
1 level tablespoon chopped fresh coriander, plus 12 extra whole leaves
4oz (100g) butter
1½lbs (700g) carrots, finely grated
6 medium eggs, separated

### For filling:
6 medium eggs, hard-boiled and shelled
1 bunch of cress, stalks removed
7oz (200g) good-quality mayonnaise

## METHOD

Line a 13" x 9" (33cm x 23cm) Swiss roll tin with baking parchment. Sprinkle the Parmesan over the paper, then scatter the whole coriander leaves on top. Melt the butter in a frying pan. Add the carrots and cook gently for 10 minutes or until soft. Drain well, tip into a bowl and beat in the egg yolks. Season well. Whisk the egg whites in a clean bowl until stiff, then fold into the mixture with the chopped coriander. Spoon into the prepared tin and spread evenly. Bake at 400°F/200°C/ Gas 6 for 10–12 minutes or until golden brown and springy to the touch. Cool.

For the filling, chop the eggs, put in a bowl with the mayonnaise and cress and mix well, seasoning with salt and pepper to taste. Turn the roulade out onto a sheet of greaseproof paper and spread with the filling, leaving a ½" (1cm) border. Beginning from a short side and using the greaseproof paper to help, roll up. Trim the edges to neaten. Chill until ready to serve, then cut into slices.

*Easy on the conscience for those counting calories...*

# WATERCRESS Roulade with Chopped BACON & MUSHROOMS

(serves 6)

## INGREDIENTS
### For roulade:
1pt (600ml) milk
1 stick of celery and 1 onion
1 bunch of watercress (without stalks)
2oz (50g) butter
2oz (50g) flour
4 large eggs, separated
Salt and pepper
Watercress or parsley for decoration

### For filling:
4oz (100g) cream cheese
¼pt (150ml) double cream
6 grilled streaky bacon rashers
4oz (100g) mushrooms, finely chopped

## METHOD
Bring milk to boil with celery and onion (skinned and halved). Leave to cool. Strain into jug and add watercress. Liquidise. Line baking tray with non-stick parchment. Melt butter in saucepan and stir in flour. Cook for one minute then add milk gradually, whisking like mad so there are no lumps. Bring to boil and season. Cool for 10 minutes. Then beat in egg yolks, one at a time. Whisk egg whites until stiff and fold into watercress mixture. Pour onto lined baking tray and smooth. Bake at 350°F/180°C/Gas 4 for about 20 minutes.

Meanwhile, fry mushrooms in a little butter. Grill streaky bacon and chop. Mix cream cheese and cream together, add bacon and mushrooms. Take roulade out of oven and cover with a damp tea towel and leave to cool. To serve, turn roulade out onto non-stick baking paper on table. Carefully tear off lining paper and spread with bacon and mushroom mixture. Roll up and decorate with watercress or parsley.

# SMOKED SALMON
# & HERB Roulade

(serves 6-8)

## INGREDIENTS
6oz (150g) smoked salmon, chopped
1 Boursin herb cheese
1 bag of herby salad
1oz (25g) butter
1oz (25g) plain flour
½pt (300ml) warm milk
2oz (50g) grated fresh Parmesan
2 tablespoons chopped fresh parsley
4 large eggs (separated)
2 tablespoons chopped fresh dill
¼pt (150ml) crème fraîche
Salt and pepper

## METHOD
Place butter, flour and warm milk in saucepan and
whisk like mad until thick. Stir in egg yolks, Parmesan,
chopped parsley, dill and salt and pepper. Whisk egg
whites until stiff and fold into egg mixture. Pour onto
a buttered 13" x 11" (33cm x 28cm) Swiss roll tin and
bake at 350°F/180°C/Gas 4 for about 12-15 minutes.
Leave covered with greaseproof paper for 15 minutes.
Tip out onto greaseproof paper sprinkled with a little
Parmesan. Mix together crème fraîche and Boursin
cheese, spread over roulade. Sprinkle with smoked
salmon pieces and roll up. Leave to firm up and cool.
Sprinkle with rest of Parmesan and serve surrounded
by a herby salad and tomatoes.

# CHOCOLATE Roulade
# with a CREAM & CHESTNUT filling

(serves 6-8)

## INGREDIENTS
### For roulade:
5 egg yolks
5 egg whites
3 tablespoons cocoa plus two
tablespoons for dusting
4oz (100g) icing sugar
1 chocolate flake or berries
for decoration

### For Chestnut filling:
¾pt (450ml) whipped cream
4 large tablespoons chestnut
purée
3 large tablespoons icing sugar

## METHOD
Soften chestnut purée by beating
together with icing sugar. Fold
into whipped cream. Beat yolks
until thick, add sugar and beat
again. Add cocoa powder and
beat. Fold in stiffly beaten egg
whites. Pour onto baking tray
9" x 12" (23cm x 30cm), lined
with baking parchment. Bake at
350°F/180°C/Gas 4 for about
20 minutes. Cool. Turn out onto
baking parchment dusted with
cocoa. Peel off parchment then
spread with whipped chestnut
cream. Gently slide onto platter
and dust with icing sugar.
Decorate with flake or berries.

*Coffee, chocolate and men –
the richer the better.*

*A dream for choc-o-holics, a nightmare for those watching their waistline!*

# LEMON Roulade with BLACKBERRIES

(serves 6-8)

## INGREDIENTS

**For roulade:**
6 eggs, separated
4oz (100g) caster sugar
Grated rind of 1 lemon
2 teaspoons lemon juice

**For Blackberry filling:**
Punnet blackberries
½pt (300ml) double cream
2 tablespoons icing sugar,
plus extra for dusting

## METHOD

Beat egg yolks with sugar until pale
and creamy. Add lemon juice and the
rind. Whisk the egg whites until soft
peaks, then fold into egg yolk mixture.
Transfer to a lined Swiss roll baking
tray 9" x 12" (23cm x 30cm), and bake
at 350°F/180°C/Gas 4 for 20 minutes.
Cool. Turn out onto baking parchment
dusted with icing sugar. Whip double
cream with 2 tablespoons of icing
sugar. Spread over meringue and
sprinkle with blackberries. Carefully roll
up with help of parchment paper. Slide
gently onto platter and serve with a
raspberry coulis.

*Kenny's recipe – perfection!*

# LEMON MERINGUE Roulade with a MANGO & PASSION FRUIT Sauce

(serves 6)

## INGREDIENTS

**For roulade:**
5 egg whites
5oz (125g) caster sugar
1 teaspoon cornflour
½pt (300ml) double cream
6 dessertspoons lemon curd

**For mango and passion fruit sauce:**
1 large ripe mango
Juice of 1 large orange
2 ripe wrinkly passion fruit
Icing sugar to taste

## METHOD

Whisk egg whites until stiff. Add one tablespoon caster sugar and whisk. Gradually add rest of sugar and cornflour. Spoon meringue onto Swiss roll tin lined with non-stick baking paper and level surface. Bake at 200°F/100°C/ Gas ¼ for 45 minutes. Cool for 1 hour. Whip cream and fold in lemon curd. Turn meringue onto baking paper dusted with icing sugar. Peel off paper carefully. Spread with lemon curd mixture and roll up. Dust with icing sugar and serve with mango and passion fruit sauce.

For sauce, peel, stone and slice mango. Purée in processor with orange juice. Sieve. Halve and scoop out seeds of passion fruit. Stir into mango and add icing sugar to taste.

*Divine!*

# HAZELNUT ROULADE filled with DULCE DE LECHE, BANANAS and WHIPPED CREAM

(serves 6)

## INGREDIENTS
6 eggs, separated
6ozs (175g) caster sugar + 1oz (25g) for topping
1oz (25g) self-raising flour
1oz (25g) cocoa powder
4ozs (100g) packet chopped roasted hazelnuts
½pt (300ml) double cream, whipped
1 jar Dulce de Leche
2 bananas (chopped)

## METHOD
Line a Swiss roll tin with buttered baking parchment. Grind 3½ozs (90g) of the hazelnuts by blitzing with flour and cocoa powder in processor. In mixer, whisk egg yolks with 6ozs (175g) caster sugar until light and fluffy. Whisk egg whites until firm peaks. Add the ground hazelnut mixture to egg yolks and gently fold in the whisked whites. Spread mixture into prepared Swiss roll tin. Bake for about 15 minutes at 325°F/170°C/Gas 3. Pulse remaining ½oz (10g) chopped hazelnuts with 1oz (25g) caster sugar until ground, and scatter onto hot roulade. Allow to cool in tin before filling and rolling.

To fill, turn roulade onto a sheet of baking parchment and gently peel off baking paper. Spread with ⅓ jar Dulce de Leche. Mix chopped banana into the whipped cream and spread evenly over roulade, followed by more Dulce de Leche (save a little for serving). Roll the roulade up tightly and refrigerate. To serve, warm remainder of Dulce de Leche (or some caramel sauce) and drizzle round and over roulade.

*There are never any leftovers!*

# The Main Event

# Fresh Fish

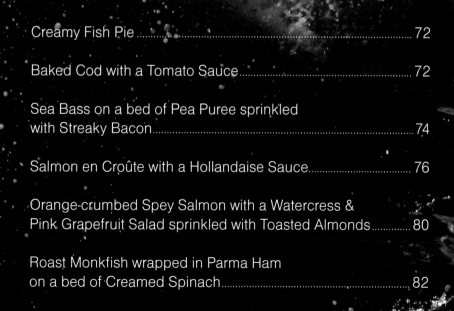

# Creamy FISH Pie

(serves 6)

## INGREDIENTS
2lbs (900gm) mixed fish – salmon,
haddock, whiting, cod, prawns
½pt (300ml) semi-skimmed milk
1 bay leaf
1oz (25g) butter
1oz (25g) flour
3oz (75g) Philadelphia (light)
2 sheets filo pastry
Chopped parsley

## METHOD
Remove skin and bones from fish.
Pour milk into pan and put in bay leaf.
Add fish and simmer for 7–8 minutes
until just cooked. Remove the fish
from milk, strain liquid and leave.
Flake fish and spoon into 3 pt (1.75
litres) ovenproof pie dish. Place butter,
flour and warm poaching liquid into
pan and stir like mad until simmering
and thickened. Stir in Philadelphia
and parsley, season and pour over
fish. Brush edge of pie dish with olive
oil. Unroll filo pastry and lay a sheet
of pastry over pie dish. Brush with
olive oil then repeat with other sheet.
Scrunch up the overhanging pastry,
fold onto pie's surface and brush with
olive oil. Bake at 375°F/190°C/Gas 5
for about 30–35 minutes until golden.

# Baked COD with a TOMATO Sauce

(serves 4)

## INGREDIENTS
4 skinless cod fillets
1 onion, finely chopped
1oz (25g) butter
1 pt (600ml) double cream
4 tablespoons tomato purée
12 slices streaky bacon
(fried/grilled and chopped)
2oz (50g) melted butter
Sprinkle of lemon juice
3oz (75g) grated Parmesan cheese

## METHOD
Place fillets of cod on baking tray
covered with foil. Season, brush
with melted butter and sprinkle
with lemon juice. Place in oven
and cook at 350°F/180°C/
Gas 4 for about 10 minutes until
cooked. Meanwhile melt butter
in pan and fry onions gently until
soft. Add tomato purée, mix in
cream, season and heat. Place
cod in ovenproof dish and pour
tomato sauce over. Sprinkle
with grated Parmesan and bake
300°F/180°C/Gas 4 for about 10
minutes. Sprinkle with chopped
bacon and serve with Basmati rice.

Dead easy.

Baked COD with a TOMATO Sauce

# SEA BASS on a bed of PEA Purée sprinkled with STREAKY BACON

(serves 4)

## INGREDIENTS
4 fillets of sea bass
(skin on, scaled and boned)
10 slices of fried streaky bacon
1 lemon

**For pea purée:**
16oz (450g) frozen peas
Few mint leaves

## METHOD
Score sea bass skin and place onto non-stick baking sheet, flesh side down. Grill for about 5 minutes until flesh starts to flake. Meanwhile, boil frozen peas in pan with enough water to cover, for about 6 minutes, then blend with a few mint leaves in liquidiser. Season. If too thick add a little cream. Warm gently before serving. To serve, place a pool of pea purée on plate, top with sea bass and sprinkle crispy bacon and parsley over. Serve with quarters of lemon.

The best.

# SALMON en Croûte with a HOLLANDAISE Sauce

(serves 6)

## INGREDIENTS

1¼lbs (550g) fresh salmon fillet
(skinned and boned)
2oz (50g) butter
1 egg yolk
½pt (300ml) double cream
8oz (225g) sliced mushrooms
1 packet (1lb/454g) puff pastry
(bought puff pastry is excellent
and a tremendous time saver)
Salt and pepper

### For hollandaise sauce:
4 egg yolks
1 tablespoon water
2 tablespoons lemon juice
6oz (150g) melted butter
Salt and pepper

## Clare's tip:

*If the Hollandaise curdles, add
an ice cube and whisk like mad!
Hollandaise keeps perfectly for
hours in a thermos flask.*

## METHOD

Whizz 10oz (275g) salmon in
food processor with butter, egg
yolk and salt and pepper. Add
cream. Roll out pastry into large
oblong. Place salmon mixture
on top of the pastry in a much
smaller oblong (to allow room
for folding up). Top mixture with
chunks of fresh salmon 10oz
(275g), then sliced mushrooms,
salt and pepper and ½oz (12g)
butter cut into small pieces. Fold
up pastry to form a parcel and if
possible shape into a fish. Egg
wash and make holes in the top.
Bake for 25 minutes in hot oven
425°F/210°C/Gas 7. Serve with a
Hollandaise sauce.

### To make hollandaise sauce:
Whisk egg yolks, water and lemon
juice in a bowl over hot water.
Pour in melted butter and whisk
until thick.

MAINS

*Impressive and a
talking point.*

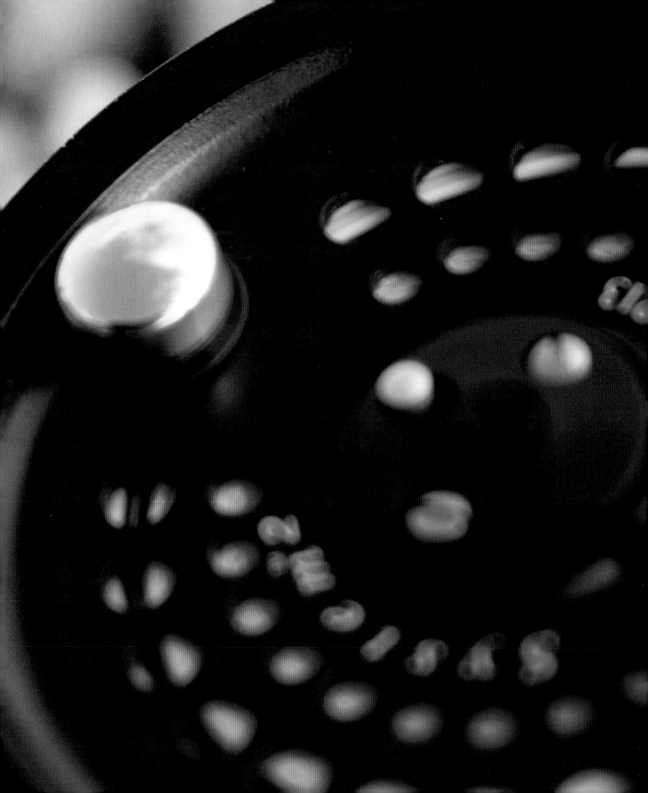

# ORANGE–crumbed Spey SALMON with a WATERCRESS & Pink GRAPEFRUIT Salad sprinkled with Toasted ALMONDS

(serves 6)

## INGREDIENTS
6 boneless skinless salmon fillets
4oz (100g) fresh breadcrumbs
3 tablespoons olive oil plus extra
for greasing
Grated zest and juice of 1 orange
6 tablespoons chopped parsley

### For salad:
2 bags watercress
2 pink grapefruits
2 tablespoons runny honey
1 tablespoon wholegrain mustard
4–5 tablespoons extra
virgin olive oil
3oz (75g) flaked almonds, toasted
(place almonds in small saucepan
and toast until they start to brown-
set aside)
1 red chilli, de-seeded and finely
chopped

*Always popular
and so easy.*

## METHOD
Mix together in a bowl breadcrumbs, oil, juice and zest of orange, half the parsley and season. Place salmon on baking sheet lined with slightly greased foil. Press orange crumbs onto each fillet firmly. Bake at 350°-400°F/180°C-200°C/ Gas 6 for about 12–15 minutes until cooked. Meanwhile make dressing for watercress salad. Mix honey and mustard in bowl and season. Halve and squeeze one of the grapefruits and add to mixture. Add olive oil slowly stirring all the time. Peel the other grapefruit and remove each segment minus its pith. Mix grapefruit with chilli then toss with watercress. Drizzle half the dressing over top. To serve, heap salad onto serving plates, place salmon fillet alongside. Sprinkle with toasted almonds and drizzle the rest of the dressing over top.

# Roast MONKFISH wrapped in PARMA HAM on a bed of Creamed SPINACH

(serves 4)

## INGREDIENTS
4 monkfish fillets
2oz (50g) melted butter
8 sage leaves
12 slices Parma ham
2 packets creamed spinach (Waitrose)
Parsley to garnish
Salt and pepper

## METHOD
Brush each monkfish fillet with butter and season. Place 2 large sage leaves on each fillet and wrap with 3 slices of Parma ham on each. Brush with melted butter and cook in oven at 400°F/180°C/Gas 6 for 12–15 minutes until firm to the touch. Meanwhile warm creamed spinach. To serve make a pool of creamed spinach, top with sliced monkfish and sprinkle with parsley. Serve with new potatoes.

*Lovely , crunchy
and interesting.*

# Chicken

# CHICKEN Breasts with quick MUSHROOM Sauce

**(serves 2)**

## INGREDIENTS
2 chicken breasts
1 tablespoon oil
½oz (15g) butter
10oz (275g) mushrooms, sliced
4fl oz (100ml) white wine
4fl oz (100ml) double cream
2 tablespoons parsley leaves

## METHOD
Heat oil in frying pan, season chicken and fry for 2 minutes on either side. Place on baking sheet in oven and bake at 350°F/180°C/Gas 4 for 20 minutes. Melt butter in frying pan, add mushrooms and salt and pepper. Fry until soft, add wine and bring to boil for a few minutes. Reduce heat and stir in cream, simmering until sauce has thickened. Stir in parsley and pour over chicken breasts. Serve with new potatoes and puréed carrot and celeriac.

MAINS

Good family supper.

# Pauline's CHICKEN

(serves 4)

## INGREDIENTS
4 chicken breasts
1 leek
1oz (25g) butter
Salt and pepper

### For velouté sauce:
1oz (25g) butter
¾oz (20g) flour
½pt (300ml) chicken stock
¼pt (300ml) milk
Salt and pepper

### Topping:
3 slices bread (crumbs)
4oz (100g) Parmesan grated

## METHOD
Fry chicken breasts gently in butter then bake in the oven for 12 minutes at 350°F/180°C/Gas 4. Set aside and keep warm. Meanwhile add chopped leeks to pan and cook until soft. Then make velouté sauce. Place all ingredients in a pan and whisk like mad until thickened. Season. Cut chicken into chunks and add to sauce. Add leeks and top with breadcrumbs and Parmesan. Place in oven for 10–15 minutes at 350°F/180°C/Gas 4 until lightly browned.

# ORANGE and CORIANDER CHICKEN

(serves 6-8)

## INGREDIENTS
4 chicken breasts (skinned and boned)
8oz (200g) long grain rice
Zest of 1 lemon
Seasoned flour
1 beaten egg
3 tablespoons olive oil

### For marinade:
Juice and zest of 1 orange
Squeeze of lemon juice

### For sauce:
Juice and zest of 1 large orange
Juice of 1 lemon
1 tablespoon fresh coriander leaves

## METHOD
Place the chicken fillets between 2 sheets of cling film and flatten with rolling pin. Remove from cling film and place in oven-proof dish. Mix marinade together, pour over chicken and leave for 1 hour. Cook rice until tender. Drain and mix in zest of 1 lemon. Cover and keep warm. Remove chicken from marinade and blot dry with kitchen paper. Toss in seasoned flour, then into beaten egg, then into the flour again. Fry in hot oil in large pan until golden brown and cooked. For the sauce, add orange juice and zest and lemon juice to pan. Bring to the boil and add coriander and salt and pepper. Slice chicken breasts diagonally and arrange on plates. Pour in the sauce and serve with lemon slice, rice and green salad.

Celebration of HM Queen Elizabeth II's
Diamond Jubilee at Ballindalloch

# Coronation CHICKEN
# The revival of an historic recipe

**(serves 6-8)**

## INGREDIENTS

2 ¼lbs (1kg) cooked chicken/
turkey breasts, chopped into
bite-sized pieces
1 tablespoon oil
1 onion thinly sliced
3 tablespoons curry paste
10oz (250g) Greek yoghurt
3 tablespoons mayonnaise
3 tablespoons mango chutney
2oz (50g) dried apricots
(chopped)
2oz (50g) sultanas
Large handful of coriander roughly
chopped or sprinkle with roasted
flaked almonds

## METHOD

Place oil in frying pan, add onion
and cook until soft. Add curry
paste and fry for 2–3 minutes.
Transfer to bowl, cool a little then
add yoghurt, mayonnaise, chutney,
chicken, apricots and sultanas.
Season to taste. Serve scattered
with coriander leaves or almonds.
Serve with a variety of salads.

*Her Majesty The Queen's
Diamond Jubilee Prayer*

*God of time and eternity,
whose Son reigns as servant, not master;
we give you thanks and praise
that you have blessed this Nation,
the Realms and Territories
with ELIZABETH,
our beloved and glorious Queen.
In this year of Jubilee,
grant her your gifts of love and joy and peace
as she continues in faithful obedience to you,
her Lord and God
and in devoted service to her lands and peoples,
and those of the Commonwealth,
now and all the days of her life;
through Jesus Christ our Lord.*

*Amen*

MAINS

# BRIE-stuffed CHICKEN with Creamy PESTO

(serves 4)

## INGREDIENTS
4 chicken breasts (skinned)
8oz (225g) Brie cheese
8 slices Parma ham
2 tablespoons green pesto (buy or make)
2 tablespoons crème fraîche

### For pesto sauce:
2oz (50g) basil leaves
½oz (12g) garlic
1oz (25g) pine nuts
5fl oz (125ml) olive oil
Salt and pepper

## METHOD
Cut sideways into each chicken breast to make a pocket. Cut Brie into 4 slices and stuff into each piece of chicken. Wrap 2 slices of Parma ham around each piece of chicken and secure with a cocktail stick. Place chicken on lightly oiled baking tray and cook at 375°F/190°C/Gas 5 for about 35 minutes or until chicken is cooked through. Remove cocktail sticks, slice and transfer to warm plate. Mix pesto with crème fraîche in a small bowl and drizzle over chicken. Serve with new potatoes and a green salad.

### To make pesto sauce:
Blend dry ingredients. Add oil until creamy.

# Pork & Ham

# Clare's PORK Chops

(serves 6)

## INGREDIENTS

8 pork chops
1 large finely chopped onion
1pt (600ml) double cream
4 tablespoons tomato purée
8 slices ham
8 dessertspoons grated cheese

## METHOD

Fry pork chops gently in butter until golden brown. Place in a flat oven proof dish and cover with a slice of ham. Fry onion in butter and place on top of pork and ham. Pour tomato purée into pan with juices, mix in cream and season. Pour over pork and sprinkle with grated cheese. Place in moderate oven 350°F/180°C/Gas 4 for 20–25 minutes. Serve with brown rice.

Igniting on a large scale!

Diamond Jubilee beacon on Ben Rinnes

# PORK fillets with a creamy PRUNE & ARMAGNAC sauce

(serves 4)

## INGREDIENTS

1 large or 2 small pork fillets
4oz (100g) butter
1 tin (15oz/425g) prunes, stoned
1 tablespoon flour
4fl oz (125ml) Armagnac
2 finely chopped onions
¼lb (100g) mushrooms
½pt (300ml) double cream
Salt and pepper

## METHOD

Slice pork into 8 pieces and flatten by beating. Roll in seasoned flour and fry lightly in butter on both sides. Arrange on oven-proof dish and keep warm. Fry onions and sliced mushrooms and sprinkle over fillets. Add Armagnac to pan and ignite carefully, standing well back from flame. Add double cream and prunes and heat gently. Pour over pork and bake at 350°F/180°C/Gas 4 for 15 minutes. Serve with wild rice.

PORK fillets with
a creamy PRUNE &
ARMAGNAC sauce

# Roast Rack of PORK with PRUNE, APPLE & APRICOT stuffing

# Roast Rack of PORK with PRUNE, APPLE & APRICOT stuffing

**(serves 4)**

## INGREDIENTS

1.8kg (6-rib) pork loin joint –
Ask your butcher to score the skin

### For stuffing:

1oz butter
1 leek (white part, diced)
1 shallot (diced)
2 Cox apples (peeled & diced)
8 prunes and 8 apricots halved
(preferably soaked)
Pinch cinnamon and ginger
Salt and pepper

### For gravy:

Glass wine
½pt stock or water
2 tablespoons of gravy granules
or cornflour

## METHOD

Make a pocket through the centre
of the loin with a sharp knife (you
can ask your butcher to do this) to
allow you to stuff the pork.

Prepare the stuffing by sweating
the leek, shallot, apple, dried fruits
and spices in the melted butter,
for several minutes. Allow to cool,
and pack into the pork loin pocket
tightly. Tie with butcher's twine.

Rub the skin with oil and salt. Place
on a trivet in roasting pan, roast
for first 30 minutes in a hot oven
400°F/200°C/Gas 6. Reduce
temperature to 350°F/180°C/Gas
4 and roast for a further 2 hours.

(As a guide cook pork joints for
30 minutes per 1lb (450g) plus 30
minutes extra).

Remove joint from oven and rest in
a warm place for 20 minutes before
cutting string and carving.

For the perfect crackling, cut
off the string and cut away the
crackling. Place on a baking tray,
inner side uppermost and place
back in a really hot oven for about
15 minutes until really crispy.

To make the gravy, tip off any fat
from the trivet, and place roasting
tin directly on stove. Add the gravy
granules or corn flour, the glass of
wine and the stock or water. Bring
it up to the boil. Simmer for a few
minutes until it thickens. Pour into a
pot, through a fine sieve. Serve with
your carved pork, roast potatoes
and vegetables.

# Collops of PORK
# with Caramelised APPLES

(serves 4-6)

## INGREDIENTS

3 pork tenderloins
2 tablespoons olive oil
½ teaspoon chopped fresh
Rosemary
Salt and pepper

**For mustard sauce:**
5fl oz (120ml) white wine
1 tablespoon Dijon mustard
4 tablespoons crème fraîche

**For caramelised apples:**
2oz (50g) butter
11oz (300g) sliced cooking
apples
4oz (100g) brown sugar

## METHOD

Sprinkle rosemary and salt and
pepper over pork on all sides.
Heat oil in large frying pan. Add
pork tenderloins and sear on both
sides until brown (about 2 minutes
per side). Place in roasting pan
and roast at 350°F/180°C/
Gas 4 for about 30 minutes.
Meanwhile make mustard sauce.
Return frying pan to heat, add
white wine, cook 1–2 minutes
until slightly reduced. Whisk in
mustard, mix in crème fraîche and
set aside. Meanwhile caramelise
apples. Melt butter in pan, add
sliced apples and sprinkle with
brown sugar. Cook until syrupy
but apples still firm (about 3–4
minutes). Slice pork diagonally
onto individual plates. Cover with
hot mustard sauce accompanied
with hot caramelised apples, new
potatoes and broad beans.

# Lamb

# Crusty LAMB with APRICOTS & WALNUTS

(serves 6)

## INGREDIENTS
2 fillets of Scottish lamb – about
7oz (175g) each
6oz (150g) finely chopped
mushrooms
8oz (225g) coarse country pâté
2–3 tablespoons olive oil
8oz (225g) dried apricots,
chopped
1 small packet chopped walnuts
or pecans
2 x 13oz (375g) packets of ready-
rolled puff pastry
8oz (225g) large spinach leaves
1 large egg, beaten
1 garlic clove, finely chopped
Salt and pepper

## METHOD
Heat 2 tablespoons olive oil in
frying pan. Sear lamb fillets all
over until browned. Remove
from pan and set aside. Fry
mushrooms and garlic lightly.
Remove from pan with slotted
spoon and set aside. Mix together
pâté, mushrooms and garlic,
chopped apricots and walnuts.
Season. Wash spinach leaves
and place in saucepan. Cook
gently until wilted. Squeeze water
out well. Cool. Place ready-rolled
pieces of puff pastry on board.
Lay spinach leaves on top. Spread
pâté mixture over spinach, then
place fillets of lamb on each and
fold into 2 neat parcels. Brush with
beaten egg and place on baking
tray. Rest in fridge for 10 minutes,
then bake at 400°F/200°C/Gas
6 for 20–25 minutes until pastry
is crusty and golden. Serve sliced
thickly with new potatoes and
mangetout.

*Unusual, and melts in the mouth.*

# Leg of LAMB stuffed with SPINACH, PINE NUTS & APRICOTS served with BÉARNAISE Sauce

(serves 6-8)

## INGREDIENTS
1 x 6lb (2.7kg) leg of lamb (boned)
1 tin 15oz (425g) apricots
1 pkt 10oz (275g) creamed spinach, frozen (Waitrose)
1 small onion, grated
2 tablespoons fresh breadcrumbs
1 lemon, grated
2oz (50g) pine nuts
Salt and pepper

### For béarnaise sauce:
½ onion, finely chopped
6 tablespoons white wine vinegar
12 black peppercorns crushed
3 sprigs fresh tarragon and thyme
6 egg yolks
12oz (300g) butter, cut into cubes
Salt

## METHOD
Chop apricots then add defrosted creamed spinach, grated onion, breadcrumbs, grated lemon and salt and pepper. Stuff lamb with mixture and sew up. If any stuffing is left over, bake it separately. Roast lamb for about 2 hours in moderate oven at 375°F/190°C/ Gas 5 on a layer of root vegetables.

Meanwhile, make Béarnaise sauce. Put onion, vinegar, peppercorns and herbs into small pan. Bring to boil and simmer for about 10 minutes. Cool and strain into bowl. Beat egg yolks into onion and herb mixture. Place the bowl over pan of simmering water. Whisk like mad until mixture begins to thicken, add butter a little at a time, still whisking, until sauce thickens. Season and serve with the roast lamb and new potatoes.

*Great for Sunday lunch.*

MAINS

*Love this.*

# Rack of Banffshire LAMB with a HERB Crust & MINT Hollandaise

(serves 4)

## INGREDIENTS

2 racks best end French-trimmed lamb - 6 ribs / 300g each
(Tesco finest range of lamb racks are superb for this recipe)
1 tablespoon olive oil
2 tablespoons Dijon mustard (For sticking herb crust to the lamb)

**For herb crust:**

3oz (75g) dried white breadcrumbs
2 tablespoons chopped parsley
1 teaspoon chopped thyme
1 teaspoon chopped rosemary
1 tablespoon lemon oil
1 clove garlic crushed

**For mint hollandaise:**

4 egg yolks
1 tablespoon water
2 tablespoons lemon juice
1 tablespoon finely chopped mint
6oz (150g) melted butter
Salt and pepper

*One of the recipes I would like to take to my desert island.*

## METHOD

Pulse herb crust ingredients for a few seconds in a food processor or mix in a bowl.

Heat the olive oil in a frying pan and sear the lamb over a hot heat until lightly browned on both sides. Place racks on a wire trivet and roast in a hot oven for 15 minutes at 425°F/220°C/Gas 7. Remove lamb from oven, and spread with mustard and press crumb mixture on top. Roast for a further 15–20 minutes depending on how pink you like your lamb. Rest in a warm place for 10 minutes before carving.

**For mint hollandaise:**

Whisk egg yolks, water and lemon juice in bowl over hot water. Pour in hot melted butter and whisk until thick. Season and add chopped mint.

**Clare's tip:**
If the Hollandaise curdles, add an ice cube and whisk like mad!

# Noisettes of LAMB with a Crispy BACON edge

(serves 4)

## INGREDIENTS
1 large or 2 small loins of lamb
6 slices streaky bacon
1 tablespoon olive oil
1 teaspoon chopped mint
1 tablespoon apricot jam
1 tablespoon wine vinegar

## METHOD
Roll loins in streaky bacon. Wrap tightly in cling film and leave in fridge for 30 minutes. Meanwhile, heat jam in pan over gentle heat. Add chopped mint and wine vinegar and heat. Keep warm. Take cling film off loins and roll in hot oil in frying pan until bacon is crispy. Take out and slice into 1" (2½ cm) noisettes. Fry noisettes both sides on high heat for about 2 minutes until golden brown. Serve the noisettes with a spoonful of apricot and mint sauce accompanied by potato dauphinois and buttered mangetout.

*Love these!*

# Venison & Game

At Ballindalloch we have
Red deer & Roe deer
for venison

# Loin of VENISON sprinkled with Roasted Flaked ALMONDS & served with a PORT and NECTARINE Sauce

(serves 6)

## INGREDIENTS

1 boned saddle of venison
(roe deer if possible)
3 tablespoons olive oil with
knob of butter
1 tablespoon flour
4oz (100g) almond flakes
(roasted in hot oven on baking tray
– watch carefully)
Salt and pepper

### For sauce:

5 nectarines
4 tablespoons port
2 tablespoons redcurrant jelly
1 tablespoon Worcestershire sauce
2oz (50g) butter
Rind and juice of 1 orange

## METHOD

Heat oil and knob of butter in frying pan. Quickly roll venison in seasoned flour. Fry for 2–3 minutes (for rare) on each side of both loins. Place on hot serving plate and keep warm. Make sauce by placing butter and rest of ingredients (except nectarines) in pan. Reduce liquid by simmering for about 15 minutes. Season, add 4 sliced nectarines and warm. Pour sauce around venison and decorate with extra nectarine and sprinkle with roasted almonds. Serve with creamed potatoes.

*Unusual and delightful.*

# Minced VENISON Cobbler

(serves 8)

## INGREDIENTS

3½lbs (1.6kg) minced venison
2 tablespoons oil
2 large onions, finely chopped
4 carrots, peeled and finely chopped
2 teaspoons Worcestershire sauce
2 tablespoons red wine vinegar
Few drops Tabasco sauce
1¼pt (700ml) venison or chicken stock
2 bay leaves
2 x 14oz (400g) cans chopped tomatoes
Pinch sugar

### For cobbler:

12oz (350g) self raising flour
½ teaspoon baking powder
½ teaspoon salt
2 tablespoons of thyme and rosemary (chopped)
8oz (225g) chilled butter in small pieces
6oz (150g) grated Cheddar cheese
Juice of 1 lemon
1 egg, lightly beaten, for glaze

## METHOD

Heat oil in large pan. Add onions, carrots and leeks and fry gently for 5–10 minutes. Then turn up heat and add minced meat, season and stir occasionally until browned. Tip out excess fat. Add Worcestershire sauce, vinegar, Tabasco, stock, bay leaves, tomatoes and sugar and bring to boil, cover then simmer for 30 minutes. Meanwhile make cobbler. Tip flour, baking powder, salt and herbs into large bowl. Add butter and rub in. Add Cheddar cheese. Make a well, add lemon juice and 4 tablespoons of water. Gently mix together to make crumbly dough. Roll out onto floured surface to ¾" (2cm) thick. Then cut into 8 rounds using a 3" (7cm) cutter. Put mince into deep gratin dish 12" x 8" (30cm x 20cm) and arrange cobblers around it. Brush cobblers with beaten egg. Place in oven and cook at 350°F/180°C/Gas 4 for 35 minutes until golden brown. Serve immediately.

*Good shooting lunch.*

# PARTRIDGES with PEARS or APPLES

**(serves 4)**

## INGREDIENTS
4 partridges
Thyme sprigs, plus extra to scatter
3oz (75g) unsalted butter
8 slices pancetta or streaky bacon
4 large pears or apples, cored
and cut into wedges
12oz (350g) shallots
18fl oz (500ml) fresh apple juice
or pear cider
2 teaspoons plain flour

*Partridge is a delicate meat and delicious with pears and apple.*

## METHOD
Blanch unpeeled shallots in boiling water for 3 minutes until soft. Drain, cool and peel away skins. Rinse partridges, pat inside and outside with kitchen paper. Season and place thyme inside partridge. Place partridges in shallow ovenproof dish and dot with half the butter. Scatter shallots around birds and roast 375°F/190°C/Gas 5 for 10 minutes. Curl slices of pancetta over birds and return to oven for further 15 minutes. Meanwhile heat half remaining butter in frying pan and gently fry the pear/apple wedges on both sides for 3–4 minutes until golden and tender. Remove to plate. Add apple juice/pear cider to pan and bring to boil. Boil rapidly until reduced by about half. Blend remaining butter with flour to make a paste. Whisk in reduced pear/apple sauce until thickened and shiny. Scatter pears around birds and pour sauce into dish. Return to oven for further 10–15 minutes until partridges are cooked. Sprinkle with extra thyme sprigs and serve with roast potatoes and purée of celeriac.

Archibald Thorburn is considered by many to be the greatest ever bird artist. This exquisite watercolour portrays Britain's indigenous partridge. Far from 'common', it has been in decline since the introduction of pesticides and changes in farming methods in the 1950s. Happily, this traditional gamebird is now in the process of recovering some of its original population.

The beautiful Woodcook by Archibald Thorburn.

# Wild DUCK Breast with Black CHERRIES

**(serves 4)**

## INGREDIENTS
4 duck breasts (skinned)
1oz (25g) softened butter
Salt and pepper

**For cherry sauce:**
4fl oz (100ml) port or red wine
2 teaspoons cornflour
2 tablespoons cherry jam
1 teaspoon soy sauce
½ teaspoon balsamic vinegar
½ tin of stoned black cherries
Salt and pepper

## METHOD
Spread a little butter over the duck breasts. Season. Place frying pan on high heat, add duck breasts and cook for 1½ minutes on each side to brown. Then place on non-stick baking tray and bake in oven 400°F/200°C/Gas 6 for 7–8 minutes. Remove from oven, cover with foil and rest. Meanwhile, make cherry sauce.

Put port, cornflour, jam, soy sauce and vinegar in pan and whisk until smooth. Bring to boil until thickened. Season and add any juice from duck breasts and black cherries. Slice duck breasts diagonally into four and fan out onto plates. Drizzle the sauce over the top. Accompany with creamed mashed potato and a mixture of green and broad beans.

*Delicious.*

# Curried PHEASANT with APPLES & SULTANAS

(serves 4)

*Good for using up old pheasant.*

## INGREDIENTS
4 pheasant breasts (skinned)
2oz (50g) butter
2 tablespoons grapeseed oil
2 large apples (peeled, cored, sliced in rings and sprinkled with lemon juice)
1½oz (35g) golden caster sugar
1oz (25g) sultanas soaked in hot water
1 onion, finely chopped
1 tablespoon mild curry powder
1 teaspoon tomato purée
1fl oz (30ml) game/chicken stock
1fl oz (30ml) dry cider
2 tablespoons créme fraîche
Salt and pepper

## METHOD
Heat half butter and 1 teaspoon of oil in frying pan. Add apple rings and sprinkle over sugar. Fry apples until caramelised then toss in drained sultanas. Set aside and keep warm. In clean frying pan add remaining butter and oil, and brown pheasant breasts quickly. Transfer to roasting tin and roast at 425°F/220°C/Gas 7 for about 10 minutes.

Meanwhile, make sauce. Pour off all fat in the pan except 1 tablespoon. Fry onion until soft. Add curry powder and tomato purée and cook for about a minute. Pour in stock and cider and stir like mad. Bring sauce to boil and reduce until it's quite thick. Season, and stir in créme fraîche. Keep warm. Take out breasts, cover with foil and rest for ten minutes, keeping warm. To serve, slice pheasant breasts diagonally, garnish with apples and sultanas and pour over sauce. Serve with Basmati rice and a mixture of broad beans and peas.

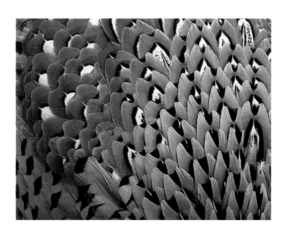

# Creamy
# PHEASANT Stroganoff

(serves 4)

## INGREDIENTS
4 pheasant breasts
1 onion, peeled and finely sliced
2oz (50g) unsalted butter
8oz (200g) mushrooms, finely sliced
(wild or porcini)
3 tablespoons brandy or whisky
(optional)
1 teaspoon French mustard
3 tablespoons crème fraîche
3fl oz (100ml) double cream
1 tablespoon tarragon, finely chopped
Paprika to taste
Parsley for decoration

## METHOD
Cut pheasant breasts into thin strips
½"(1cm) thick and 2"(5cms) long and
sprinkle with paprika. Heat half of butter in
heavy based frying pan, add onion and fry
gently until soft and golden. Remove with
a slotted spoon and set aside. Increase
heat and quickly fry meat in batches, set
aside and keep warm. Add brandy and
bubble to reduce. Place all ingredients
in pan. Lower heat and stir in mustard,
crème fraîche and cream. Heat through
and stir in tarragon. Season and serve
with rice or noodles. Garnish with parsley.

Great recipe!

CURRIED PHEASANT WITH APPLES & SULTANAS

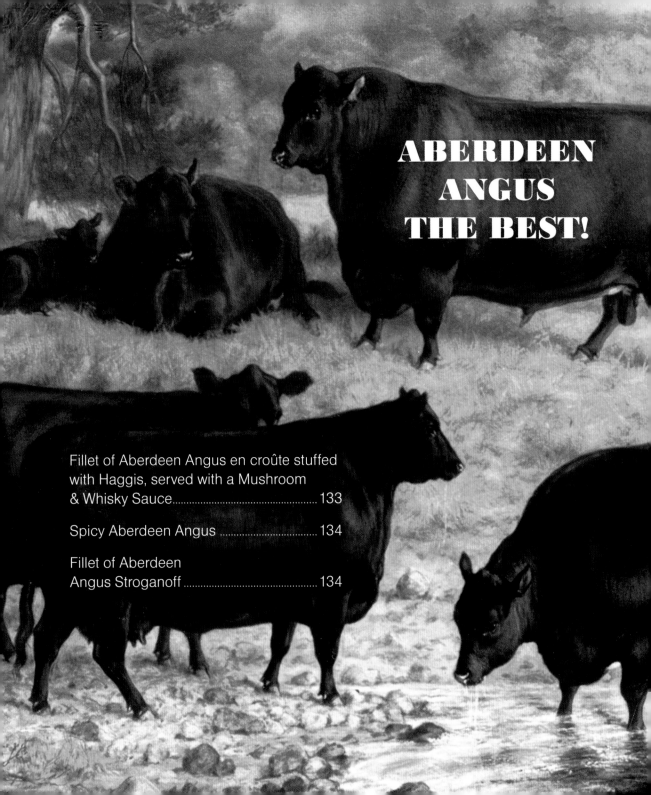

# ABERDEEN ANGUS THE BEST!

Aberdeen Angus is the best. The pedigree herd was started by my great-grandfather, Sir George Macpherson-Grant of Ballindalloch, in 1860. It is now the oldest herd in existence. Black castle have grazed peacefully in the 'Coo Haugh' beside the Castle for centuries. This beautiful race of cattle is directly descended from the native cattle found in the North East of Scotland and derives its origins from the old 'Doddies' of Angus and the 'Hummlies' from Buchan. They were all hardy, black hornless cattle whose presence in the North East of Scotland goes back to the 12th century.

Today under the stewardship of Mrs Macpherson-Grant Russell the black cattle still flourish in their serene setting beside the river Avon and are still winning prizes.

Ballindalloch 'Erica'
The champion of the north 2011.

# Fillet of ABERDEEN ANGUS en croûte stuffed with HAGGIS, served with a MUSHROOM & WHISKY Sauce

(serves 6)

## INGREDIENTS
1lb 12oz (750g) fillet of Aberdeen Angus beef
12oz (350g) wild and cultivated mushrooms, finely chopped
1oz (25g) butter
2 shallots, finely chopped
Squeeze of lemon juice
2 tablespoons flat leaf parsley
Groundnut oil
14oz (400g) puff pastry
1 roll of haggis
1 tablespoon Dijon mustard
1 medium egg (lightly beaten)
Salt and pepper

### For mushroom & whisky sauce:
2oz (50g) butter
1 onion, peeled and finely sliced
4oz (100g) mushrooms, sliced
1 tablespoon whisky (optional)
¼pt (150ml) double cream
2 teaspoons chopped parsley
(for decoration)

## METHOD
Melt butter in pan, add finely chopped shallots and cook until soft. Add finely chopped mushrooms and salt and pepper.

Fry gently for 5–6 minutes. Transfer to bowl, stir in parsley and lemon juice, then cool. Brush fillet all over with oil. Season and seal for a minute each side in pan. Transfer to plate and cool. Roll out pastry thinly on floured work surface. Slice and spread haggis over middle of pastry length and width of fillet. Spread mushrooms on top of haggis. Brush top of fillet with mustard and place mustard side down on top of mushrooms. Parcel the fillet up, paint one of the long edges with beaten egg and both of the short sides. Parcel together, trimming any excess pastry off. Place, sealed edges down, on roasting tin. Use pastry trimmings to decorate top and brush all over with beaten egg. Bake at 425°F/220°C/Gas 8 for about 30 minutes until golden. Leave to rest for 10 minutes then carve. Serve with mushroom sauce.

### For mushroom & whisky sauce:
Fry onions and mushrooms in butter in pan until soft. Add whisky, cream, and salt and pepper. Simmer for a few minutes and serve with fillet of beef sprinkled with a little parsley.

# Spicy ABERDEEN ANGUS

(serves 3-4)

## INGREDIENTS
1lb 2oz (500g) minced
Aberdeen Angus beef
1 tablespoon oil
1 large onion, finely
chopped
14oz (400g) tin chopped
tomatoes
15oz (420g) tin kidney
beans in chilli sauce
1 teaspoon chilli paste
Handful of fresh coriander,
finely chopped
Greek yoghurt to serve

## METHOD
Gently heat oil in large
saucepan, then cook onion
until soft. Add beef and stir.
Season well, add tomatoes,
kidney beans and chilli
paste. Mix well and cook
for about 40 minutes. Serve
with Basmati rice and a
green salad.

# Fillet of ABERDEEN ANGUS Stroganoff

(serves 4)

## INGREDIENTS
1½lbs (700g) fillet Aberdeen Angus beef
1 onion, peeled and finely sliced
2oz (50g) unsalted butter
8oz (200g) mushrooms, finely sliced
(wild or porcini)
3 tablespoons brandy or whisky
(optional)
1 teaspoon French mustard
3 tablespoons crème fraîche
3fl oz (100ml) double cream
1 tablespoon tarragon, finely chopped &
paprika to taste
Parsley for decoration

## METHOD
Cut fillet into thin strips ½"(1cm) thick and
2"(5cms) long and sprinkle with paprika.
Heat half of butter in heavy based frying
pan, add onion and fry gently until soft
and golden. Remove with a slotted spoon
and set aside. Increase heat and quickly
fry meat in batches, set aside and keep
warm. Add brandy, set alight and let
bubble to reduce. Place all ingredients
in pan. Lower heat and stir in mustard,
crème fraîche and cream. Heat through
and stir in tarragon. Season and serve
with rice or noodles. Garnish with parsley.

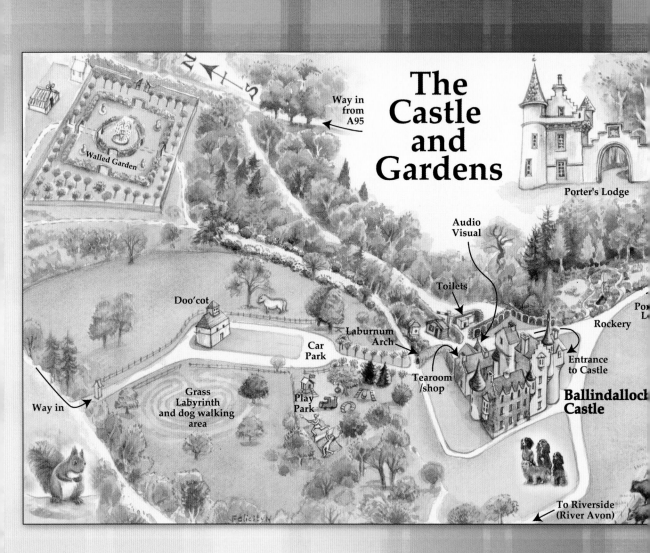

# The Castle and Gardens

Walled Garden

Way in from A95

Porter's Lodge

Audio Visual

Toilets

Doo'cot

Laburnum Arch

Car Park

Rockery

Po... L...

Entrance to Castle

Tearoom /shop

**Ballindalloch Castle**

Way in

Grass Labyrinth and dog walking area

Play Park

To Riverside (River Avon)

FelicityM

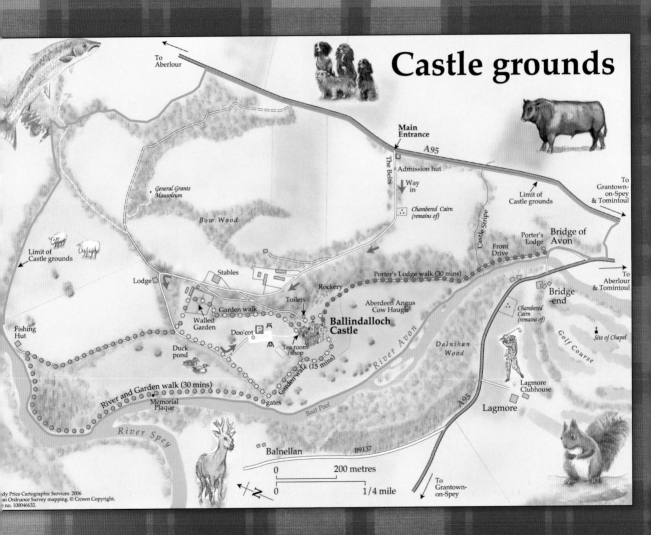

# Castle grounds

To Aberlour

Main Entrance

A95

The Belts

Admission hut

Way in

General Grants Mausoleum

Chambered Cairn *(remains of)*

Bow Wood

Castle Stripe

Limit of Castle grounds

Limit of Castle grounds

Porter's Lodge

Bridge of Avon

Fishing Hut

Lodge

Stables

Rockery

Porter's Lodge walk (30 mins)

Front Drive

To Grantown-on-Spey & Tomintoul

Garden walk

Toilets

Aberdeen Angus Cow Haugh

**Ballindalloch Castle**

Bridge-end

Chambered Cairn *(remains of)*

Site of Chapel

To Aberlour & Tomintoul

Golf Course

Walled Garden

Doo'cot

Duck pond

P

Tea room / shop

River Avon

Dalnihan Wood

River and Garden walk (30 mins)

Memorial Plaque

Garden walk (15 mins)

gates

Boat Pool

Lagmore Clubhouse

Lagmore

A95

River Spey

Balnellan

B9137

0        200 metres

0        1/4 mile

To Grantown-on-Spey

N

dy Price Cartographic Services. 2006
on Ordnance Survey mapping. © Crown Copyright.
no. 100046632.

Let us be grateful to people who make us happy; they are the charming gardeners who make our souls blossom

Marcel Proust

BEST
POTATO
lb
5 £2.00

# GREENS are GOOD for you

# Baked VEGETABLES (baked in a foil parcel)

**(serves 4)**

## INGREDIENTS

12oz (350g) carrots, scrubbed
and cut into 1" (2.5cm) chunks
12oz (350g) parsnips, scrubbed
and cut into 2" (5cm) chunks
12oz (350g) small red potatoes,
unpeeled and each potato cut into
8 wedges
1 medium red onion, peeled and
cut into 8, through the root
1 head celery, trimmed and cut
into ¾" (2cm) chunks
5 tablespoons vinaigrette dressing
2 sprigs thyme
2 sprigs rosemary
1 bay leaf
Season

## METHOD

Preheat oven to 400°F/200°C/
Gas 6. Fold a piece of foil 36" x
12" (90cm x 30cm) in half and
lay one half along the length of
a deep roasting tray 14" x 11"
(35cm x 28cm). Brush with a
little vinaigrette and lay all the
vegetables on the foil. Season
well. Add sprigs of herbs and bay
leaf, then spoon the remaining
vinaigrette over the vegetables,
making sure they get a good
all-over coating. Now you can
fold the other half of the foil,
turning over the edges to seal
all around. This makes a parcel
with some air space between the
foil and vegetables. Place tray in
preheated oven, one shelf above
the middle, for 45 minutes. To
serve, carefully unwrap the foil
and tip the vegetables into a warm
serving dish.

# BROCCOLI & CAULIFLOWER au Gratin

(serves 4-6)

## INGREDIENTS

8oz (225g) broccoli
8oz (225g) cauliflower
2oz (50g) butter
2oz (50g) plain flour
A pinch of dry mustard powder
A pinch of cayenne pepper
1pt (600ml) milk
3oz (75g) grated Gruyère cheese
1oz (25g) grated Parmesan cheese
1 tablespoon fresh white breadcrumbs
1 tablespoon grated Cheddar cheese

## METHOD

Cook broccoli and cauliflower in boiling salted water for about 4 minutes until just tender. Drain well and place in ovenproof dish. Place butter, flour, mustard powder, cayenne pepper and milk in pan over heat and whisk like mad until it thickens. Simmer for 2 minutes then stir in Gruyère and Parmesan cheese to melt. Pour over broccoli and cauliflower. Sprinkle with breadcrumbs and Cheddar cheese and grill until golden. Serve immediately.

# RED CABBAGE with APPLES & BEETROOT

(serves 4)

## INGREDIENTS
2lbs (900g) red cabbage
1lb (450g) chopped onions
1lb (450g) cooking apples, peeled, cored and chopped
4 raw beetroot peeled and cut into wedges
1 clove of garlic chopped very small
Freshly grated nutmeg
¼ teaspoon ground cinnamon
¼ teaspoon ground cloves
3 tablespoons brown sugar
3 tablespoons wine vinegar
½oz (12g) butter
Salt and pepper

## METHOD
Throw away tough outer leaves of cabbage. Cut into quarters and remove hard stalk. Shred cabbage finely. In large ovenproof dish arrange a layer of shredded cabbage, seasoned with salt and pepper, then a layer of chopped onions, apples and beetroot with a sprinkling of garlic, spices and sugar in between until everything has been used up. Pour in wine vinegar, add butter, place lid on casserole and cook slowly in oven at 300°F/150°C/Gas 2 for 1½-2 hours, stirring everything around once or twice during cooking.

# BROAD BEANS and MANGETOUT sprinkled with PINE NUTS

(serves 4)

## INGREDIENTS
8oz (225g) beans
8oz (225g) mangetout
1oz (25g) butter
Pine nuts to garnish

## METHOD
Remove beans from pod. Bring large pan of salted water to boil. Cook beans for 4-5 minutes, adding mangetout 1 minute before the end. Drain. Place in ovenproof dish. Dot with butter and sprinkle with pine nuts.

# BRUSSELS SPROUTS sprinkled with CHESTNUTS & CRISPY BACON

(serves 4)

## INGREDIENTS
2 lbs 12oz (1.25 kg) Brussels sprouts, trimmed
8oz (225g) vacuum packed chestnuts
2oz (50g) butter
6 rashers streaky bacon

## METHOD
Bring large pan of salted water to boil. Tip in sprouts, bring to boil and cook for about 10 minutes. Meanwhile place streaky bacon in frying pan and fry until crispy. Add chestnuts and toss around for a few minutes. Drain cooked sprouts and place in ovenproof dish. Sprinkle bacon and chestnuts on top, season and serve with a knob of butter.

# PARSNIPS & POTATO Gratin

(serves 4-6)

## INGREDIENTS
1lb (450g) parsnips, peeled and trimmed
1lb (450g) potatoes, peeled and trimmed
1oz (25g) butter
1pt (600m) double cream
2oz (50g) grated cheddar cheese
1 tablespoon fresh thyme leaves (optional)
Salt and pepper

## METHOD
Parboil potatoes and parsnips, for 10–15 minutes. Drain. Cool and slice. Butter ovenproof dish and arrange potatoes and parsnips in layers, seasoning well. Scatter over thyme, pour over cream and top with cheese. Bake at 400°F/200°C/Gas 6 for 20–25 minutes until golden brown.

# COURGETTES & TOMATO au Gratin

**(serves 2-4)**

## INGREDIENTS
4 courgettes, sliced
2 tablespoons olive oil
4oz (100g) cheddar cheese, sliced
4 large tomatoes, peeled and sliced
4 level tablespoons grated
Parmesan cheese
1 tablespoon chopped fresh basil
Salt and pepper

## METHOD
Heat oil in frying pan, add sliced courgettes and fry until golden brown on each side. Then arrange layers of courgette, cheese slices and sliced tomatoes in heatproof dish. Sprinkle on grated Parmesan and salt and pepper. Bake in oven for about 30 minutes at 375°F/190°C/Gas 5.

# Creamed SPINACH

**(serves 8)**

*Always popular and delicious with egg and fish recipes.*

## INGREDIENTS
1oz (25g) butter
1 onion finely chopped
2 tablespoons flour
7fl oz (200ml) full fat milk
2 x 8oz (200g) bags spinach
3½fl oz (100ml) single cream
Grated fresh nutmeg

## METHOD
Heat butter in pan, add onion and cook for 5 minutes until soft. Stir in flour and cook for 2 minutes and then slowly start to pour in milk. Whisk like mad until sauce thickens. Meanwhile place spinach in colander. Pour over kettle of boiling water until leaves wilt. Place spinach in clean tea towel and squeeze out any excess liquid. Then chop roughly and stir into white sauce. Add cream and salt and pepper. Gently heat again. Place in an ovenproof dish and finely grate over some nutmeg.

# Creamy POTATO, BACON & CHEESE Mash

(serves 2)

## INGREDIENTS
3 large potatoes
4 rashers streaky bacon
(grilled until crispy)
1fl oz (25ml) cream
1fl oz (25ml) milk
1 bunch of chives
1oz (25g) butter
1 teaspoon English mustard
4oz (100g) Cheddar cheese
(grated)
Salt and pepper

## METHOD
Peel potatoes and bring to the boil in salted water. Simmer for 20 minutes until cooked. Warm cream, milk and chopped chives in pan over low heat for 5 minutes. Drain potatoes and mash while slowly adding cream mix, butter and mustard. Fold in chopped crispy bacon and cheese. Season and serve.

# Crispy PARSNIPS with PARMESAN

(serves 6-8)

## INGREDIENTS
2¾ lbs (1.25kg) parsnips
2oz (50g) freshly grated
Parmesan
6oz (150g) plain flour
Groundnut oil for baking
Knob of butter
Salt and pepper

## METHOD
Mix flour, Parmesan and salt and pepper in a bowl and set aside. Peel parsnips, halve and quarter lengthways, cutting out any woody bits. Cut into small chunks. Place in a pan of salted boiling water with lid on for about 3 minutes. Drain in colander, then dip with tongs while hot into flour and cheese mixture. Coat well and then place in roasting tin heated with groundnut oil and bake at 400°F/200°C/Gas 6 for about 20 minutes basting several times. Drain off fat and continue to bake for a further 15–20 minutes until crisp and golden.

# MANGETOUT & PEAS
## sprinkled with
# PINE NUTS

**(serves 4-6)**

*Looks really pretty and as if you are in the middle of podding peas!*

## INGREDIENTS
6oz (150g) mangetout (topped and tailed)
6oz (150g) frozen peas
2oz (50g) butter
Pine nuts for garnish

## METHOD
Boil peas in water for a couple of minutes. Drain and keep warm. Melt butter in frying pan, add mangetout and toss them around for about 2–3 minutes until coated in butter and cooked. Place in ovenproof dish and add peas. Sprinkle with pine nuts.

# MAPLE & WALNUT CARROTS

**(serves 8)**

## INGREDIENTS
2¼lbs (1kg) baby carrots
1 tablespoon olive oil
4 tablespoons maple syrup
1oz (25g) chopped walnuts

## METHOD
Place carrots in roasting tin, drizzle with olive oil. Cover with foil and roast for 10 minutes at 400°F/200°C/Gas7. Remove foil and roast for 20 minutes more. Drizzle with maple syrup and scatter over the walnuts. Return to oven and bake for another 10 minutes until carrots are soft and golden and walnuts are roasted.

## Purée of Baby BROAD BEANS sprinkled with CRISPY BACON

**(serves 2 greedy people!)**

*Probably only for those who have a garden and can pick the broad beans fresh.*

### INGREDIENTS
2lbs (900g) shelled broad beans
1oz (25g) butter
2½fl oz (60ml) single cream
Freshly grated nutmeg
4 rashers streaky bacon
(fried and chopped)
Salt and pepper

### METHOD
Place beans in boiling salted water. Simmer for 4–6 minutes until tender. Drain well. Place in liquidiser with butter, cream, freshly grated nutmeg and salt and pepper. Whizz to a purée and sprinkle with chopped streaky bacon.

## Puree of CARROT & CELERIAC

**(serves 4)**

### INGREDIENTS
12oz (350g) carrots, scrubbed and cut into small chunks
12oz (350g) celeriac, peeled and cut into small chunks
3 tablespoons double cream
A pinch of grated nutmeg
1 tablespoon chopped fresh chives
Salt and pepper

### METHOD
Cook carrots and celeriac separately in salted water until soft, about 20–25 minutes. Drain, whizz in liquidiser with cream, nutmeg and salt and pepper to taste. Sprinkle with chives.

# Sweet
# Tooth

Life without puddings would be unbearable – you only live once – so why not indulge and enjoy them!

Anon

PUDS

# Black CHERRY Tart with LEMON Pastry

(serves 6)

## INGREDIENTS

**For lemon pastry:**
9oz (250g) plain flour
(extra for dusting)
2oz (50g) icing sugar, sieved
5oz (125g) cold butter in cubes
Grated zest of 1 lemon
1 lightly beaten large egg
1 egg white
1 tablespoon caster sugar

**For filling:**
1lb 5oz (575g) frozen stoned
black cherries
4oz (100g) caster sugar
1 tablespoon lemon juice
1 tablespoon arrowroot

## METHOD

For filling, place black cherries in
pan with sugar and lemon juice.
Bring to simmer over medium
heat, stirring occasionally. Cook
for few minutes. Mix arrowroot
with a little water until like a paste
and stir into pan. Simmer for 2–3
minutes. Remove from heat and
leave to cool.

For the pastry, make by sieving
together the flour and icing sugar
into large mixing bowl. Add butter
and lemon zest and rub together
until a fine crumbly mixture
(this can be done in the food
processor). Add beaten egg and
1 tablespoon of cold water, then
work into a ball of dough. Divide
in half and wrap in cling film. Chill
in fridge for 30 minutes, then roll
out onto floured surface into two
rounds, using one to line base and
sides of pie dish 7"–8" (18–20cm)
and one for top to cover surface of
dish, adding ¾" (2cm) overlap.

Spoon black cherry filling into
pastry-lined tin and top with
remaining pastry. Place in fridge
for about 30 minutes. Brush over
surface of pie with lightly beaten
egg and extra egg white. Sprinkle
with caster sugar and pierce a
hole in middle of top. Place in
oven 400°F/200°C/Gas 6 for
about 20–25 minutes, until the top
is golden brown. Serve with vanilla
ice-cream or crème fraîche.

*Another fantastic
Sunday lunch recipe.*

# CHOCOLATE Buttermilk
# Crème Brûlée with ORANGE Marmalade

**(serves 6)**

## INGREDIENTS
1oz (25g) good dark chocolate
6 large egg yolks
2oz (50g) caster sugar
2oz (50g) firmly packed light brown sugar
17fl oz (400ml) double cream
5fl oz (120ml) buttermilk (or thin natural
yogurt with semi-skimmed milk)
1 vanilla pod, split in half lengthways
1 tablespoon marmalade
2–3 tablespoons sugar for
sprinkling on custards

## METHOD
Whisk together egg yolks and sugar
(except sprinkling sugar). Melt together
the chocolate with 5fl oz (120ml) of the
double cream and whisk this into the egg
yolk mixture. Whisk in the remaining double
cream and buttermilk. Scrape vanilla seeds
into mixture and whisk in orange marmalade.
Pour the mixture into 6 x 4oz (100g)
ramekins. Place them in a deep baking tray
with wire rack and pour hot water so that
it comes half way up sides of ramekins.
Bake until custards just jiggle slightly -
about 60 minutes at 275°F/140°C/Gas
1. Before serving, sprinkle with sugar
and blowtorch top of each custard.

*Delicious.*

# CHOCOLATE Fondants with a WHITE CHOCOLATE Surprise

**(serves 6-8)**

## INGREDIENTS
6½oz (165g) high quality
dark chocolate (at least 70%
cocoa solids)
8 white chocolate truffles
5oz (125g) unsalted butter
9½oz (265g) caster sugar
½ teaspoon vanilla extract
4 medium free range eggs, beaten
4½oz (110g) plain flour, sifted
Melted butter for greasing
Cocoa powder for dusting
Icing sugar for dusting

## METHOD
Heat the oven to 350°F/180°C/
Gas 4. Brush 6 to 8 small ramekins
sparingly with the melted butter,
dust with the cocoa powder and
shake out the excess. Set aside.
Melt the chocolate and butter
gently in a saucepan. Remove
from the heat and stir in the sugar
and vanilla extract. Leave to cool
slightly. Whisk the eggs into the
mixture a little at a time, then fold
in the sifted flour and a little salt
until you have a smooth mixture.
Divide the mixture between the
ramekins – filling each one until
two-thirds full. Press white truffle
into middle of chocolate making
sure it is covered by the mixture.
Place them on the middle shelf
of the oven and cook for 12–15
minutes. Remove the fondants
from the oven, run a knife around
the edges, invert and tip out
on to serving plates. Dust with
a sprinkling of icing sugar and
serve immediately with half-fat
crème fraîche, if you like.

*Chocolate makes
your clothes shrink.*

# Stag's Breath CHOCOLATE Mousse with a Mountain of Profiteroles

(serves 4-6)

## INGREDIENTS

### Chocolate mousse:
6oz (150g) good plain chocolate
2½fl oz (75ml) water
½oz (12g) butter
3 eggs (separated)
Pouring cream
1 tablespoon 'Stag's Breath'
liqueur whisky

### For profiteroles:
3oz (75g) butter
7½fl oz (225ml) water
3 eggs
3oz (75g) flour
½pt (300ml) double cream
2 tablespoons Dulce de Leche

## METHOD

For mousse, melt chocolate and water together. Cool and beat in butter. Beat in egg yolks one by one and add 1 tablespoon of Stag's Breath then fold in stiffly beaten egg whites. Pour into glass bowl and leave to set.

For profiteroles, bring butter and water to boil. When bubbling, draw aside and immediately add flour all at once. Beat until smooth and paste leaves the side of pan. Cool. Whisk eggs lightly and add slowly to mixture, beating all the time until paste is smooth and shiny. Place teaspoons of paste onto damp baking sheet. Bake at 350°F/180°C/Gas 4 for 20–30 minutes until firm to touch. Place on rack to cool. Whip cream stiffly and fold in 2 tablespoons of Dulce de Leche. Open hole in profiteroles gently and fill with cream. Spread tops with a little chocolate icing (buy fondant icing sugar and add a little melted chocolate). Pile profiteroles onto top of chocolate mousse and serve immediately.

*Two old recipes that go so well together and look so elegant.*

# CHOCOLATE Trifle

(serves 6)

## INGREDIENTS
½ chocolate Swiss roll
Liqueur (to your taste)
4 bananas
1lb 2oz (500g) chocolate custard
½pt (300ml) double cream
1 chocolate Flake
(or Bournville curls)

## METHOD
Slice the Swiss roll and lay in base of large glass bowl. Sprinkle liqueur over. Slice bananas over the top and spoon the chocolate custard over. Cover with whipped cream and sprinkle with chocolate flake.

Superbly easy.

# Tangy LEMON Possets

(serves 6)

## INGREDIENTS
1pt (600ml) double cream
6oz (150g) caster sugar
Zest and juice of 4 lemons
Punnet of raspberries/blackberries

## METHOD
Place the double cream and sugar in large saucepan (you will need a large saucepan as the mixture needs to boil vigorously). Add zest of lemons to cream. Bring the mixture to a rolling boil and allow it to boil vigorously for 5 minutes, whisking occasionally. Squeeze the juice from the lemons and add to the cream. Remove from the heat and strain through a sieve. Allow mixture to cool slightly and stir initially to prevent a skin from forming. Place few raspberries/blackberries at bottom of wine glass. Divide mixture between glasses, cover and chill in fridge for a minimum of 4 hours, then allow to come back to room temperature for 10 minutes before serving. Place raspberry/blackberry on top for decoration.

*Wonderful, and perfect with blackberries.*

# COFFEE Crème Brûlées

(serves 6)

## INGREDIENTS
1pt (600ml) whipping cream
2 teaspoons instant coffee granules
4 medium egg yolks
6oz (150g) Dulce de Leche
Caster sugar for glazing

## METHOD
Preheat the oven to 300°F/150°C/Gas 2. Place the whipping cream and coffee in a pan and slowly bring to the boil. Meanwhile, mix the egg yolks and Dulce de Leche in large bowl. Remove the coffee cream from the heat, and whisk into the yolks. Pour into 6 ramekins or small coffee cups. Carefully place the dishes in a deep baking tray and pour hot water from the kettle to come two-thirds of the way up the sides of the dishes. Cover loosely with foil and bake for 40 minutes until just set, as the residual heat in the custard will continue the cooking process. Remove from the oven and water. Set aside to chill. For the glaze, sprinkle on a thin layer of caster sugar to cover the custard. Place under a pre-heated grill for 5–6 minutes until golden and glazed, or use a hand-held cook's blowtorch. Cool slightly, and serve at room temperature.

*Wow!...*

# PEAR and TOFFEE Tart

(serves 6)

## INGREDIENTS
4 large pears
8 tablespoons Dulce de Leche
8oz (225g) sheet ready rolled puff pastry

## METHOD
Quarter pears (no need to peel) and cut out cores. Place in large non stick frying pan and add Dulce de Leche. Cook over medium heat for 5 minutes. Tip pears and sauce into 8" (20cm) round non stick tart tin. Arrange pears skin side down in a circle and leave to cool for 10 minutes. Unroll puff pastry onto floured surface. Roll out a little wider than tin and lay over pears. Press down onto edge of dish. Trim excess pastry. Prick all over and place in oven 400°F/200°C/Gas 6 for 20 minutes until pastry is well risen and golden. Leave to cool for 5 minutes. Turn out onto serving plate, shake gently to loosen and lift tin off. Serve immediately with vanilla ice cream.

# LEMON Cream Parfait in BRANDY Snap Baskets with Fresh BERRIES

(serves 6-8)

*One of my favourites, and easy when 'time' is not in your vocabulary.*

## INGREDIENTS
6 egg yolks
8oz (225g) caster sugar
2 lemons, zest and juice
½pt (300ml) double cream
6 brandy snap baskets (bought)
1 punnet Scottish berries

## METHOD
Beat egg yolks with sugar until thick and creamy. Fold in zest and juice of lemons. Whip cream and fold into mixture. Freeze. Remove from freezer and serve. Place scoops of parfait into brandy snap baskets and sprinkle with Scottish berries.

# Heather HONEY Cheesecake with RASPBERRIES

**(serves 2)**

## INGREDIENTS
4 ginger biscuits
5oz (125g) full fat soft cheese
2fl oz (60ml) double cream
1 tablespoon caster sugar
2 tablespoons runny heather or
blossom honey plus 1 teaspoon
extra to add to raspberries
5oz (125g) punnet of raspberries

## METHOD
Place 2 x 3½" (9cm) metal rings
on 2 small dessert plates. Liquidise
ginger biscuits until like fine
breadcrumbs and divide between
the rings, kneading into the rings to
make a base. Place soft cheese in
bowl and whisk together with double
cream, sugar and two tablespoons
of runny honey until thick. Spoon
mixture into rings, then spread the
top flat. Chill until ready to serve.

Crush half the raspberries with a fork
with one teaspoon of runny honey,
then gently fold in the rest. Undo
ring and lift off. Spoon over the
raspberries and serve.

*Easy, quick and lovely.*

I thank thee God, that I have lived
In this great world and known its many joys:
The songs of birds, the strong sweet scent of hay,
And cooling breezes in the secret dusk;
The flaming sunsets at the close of day,
Hills and the lovely, heather-covered moors;
Music at night, and the moonlight on the sea,
The beat of waves upon the rocky shore
And wild white spray, flung high in ecstasy;
The faithful eyes of dogs, and treasured books,
The love of kin and fellowship of friends
And all that makes life dear and beautiful.
I thank Thee too, that there has come to me
A little sorrow and sometimes defeat,
A little heartache and the loneliness
That comes with parting and the word 'Good-bye';
Dawn breaking after weary hours of pain,
When I discovered that night's gloom must yield
And morning light break through to me again.
Because of these and other blessings poured
Unasked upon my wondering head,
Because I know that there is yet to come
An even richer and more glorious life,
And most of all, because Thine only Son
Once sacrificed life's loveliness for me,
I thank Thee, God, that I have lived.

# Highland BREAD & BUTTER Pudding

(serves 6-8)

## INGREDIENTS

12 slices brioche bread
2oz (50g) softened butter
3oz (75g) raisins
3oz (75g) sultanas
3 tablespoons whisky
1oz (25g) heather honey
7 egg yolks and 1 whole egg
5oz (125g) caster sugar
½pt (300ml) milk
½pt (300ml) double cream
2 teaspoons vanilla essence
2 tablespoons demerara sugar
Icing sugar for dusting

### For apricot glaze:
4oz (100g) apricot jam boiled with
2fl oz (60ml) water to make a hot
sticky glaze

## METHOD

Grease a 3 pint pudding dish
with butter. Soak the raisins and
sultanas in the whisky
for 4 hours. Spread
each slice of
bread with the
softened
butter and
a mere

scraping of heather honey. Remove the crusts and cut in half diagonally twice, creating 4 triangles per slice. Arrange the bread in layers in the prepared ovenproof dish, scattering the raisins and sultanas between the layers.

Whisk the egg yolks, extra egg and caster sugar together. Bring the milk and cream to the simmer. Pour the hot cream mixture over the egg yolks and sugar mixture. Add the vanilla essence. You now have a custard. Pour the custard over the bread and sprinkle with demerara sugar. Bake in a bain-marie (a baking tin half-filled with hot water) in a pre-heated oven at 350°F/180°C/Gas 4 for 20–30 minutes, until the pudding begins to set. When ready, remove from the water bath. Dust with some icing sugar and glaze under the grill on medium heat.

Make the apricot glaze by boiling the apricot jam and water together. Brush a thin coating of glaze over the top of the pudding. It is now ready to serve.

*Kenny's secret recipe –
light as a feather!*

**Clare's tip:**
Try adding 2oz (50g) of white
chocolate to the pudding with the milk

# MANGO Mousse

(serves 6-8)

## INGREDIENTS
2 mangoes, skinned and stoned
5 egg yolks
4ozs (100g) icing sugar
½pt (300ml) double cream
Lime juice
6 crushed brandy snaps

## METHOD
Whizz the mango flesh in processor. Whisk egg yolks and icing sugar until pale and creamy. Whip cream. Fold mango and cream into eggs. Add lime juice to taste. Pour into ramekins. Cool for 4 hours. Sprinkle with chopped mango, crushed brandy snap or Demerara sugar before serving.

Divine!

# APPLE Flan with Glazed FRUITS

(serves 4)

## INGREDIENTS

1lb 2oz (500g) puff pastry
1 egg yolk mixed with
½ teaspoon cold water
5 Cox's apples, peeled, cored and
finely sliced
½oz (12g) melted butter
Icing sugar for dusting
Raspberries, kiwi, plum to
decorate
Clotted cream or ice-cream

### For almond paste:

1oz (25g) soft butter
2oz (50g) ground almonds
1oz (25g) caster sugar
1 tablespoon self-raising flour
1 egg yolk

### For apricot glaze:

4oz (100g) apricot jam boiled with
2fl oz (60ml) water to make a hot
sticky glaze

## METHOD

Roll out pastry to ⅛"–¼" (3–5mm)
thick and cut out a 10" (25cm)
round. Place on a flat, greased
baking tray. Prick the pastry round
all over with a fork and crimp or
score the edge with diagonal lines
to form a border. Brush the pastry
with egg yolk mixture and chill.

Meanwhile, make almond paste by
mixing all ingredients together to
make a smooth paste, and spread
onto chilled pastry circle. Arrange
sliced apples in a circular pattern
and dust with icing sugar.

Bake in a hot oven at
425°F/220°C/Gas 7 for 25
minutes until cooked and golden
on the edges.

Garnish with fruits (raspberries,
kiwi, etc) and brush with hot
apricot glaze. Serve with chilled
clotted cream or ice cream.

*A superb Sunday lunch recipe.*

# PASSION FRUIT & HONEYCOMB Parfait

(serves 4)

## INGREDIENTS
4 large passion fruits, pulped
2 large free range egg yolks
1¼oz (30g) golden caster sugar
7fl oz (180ml) double cream, lightly whipped
2 x 4oz (100g) Crunchie bars

## METHOD
To make parfait, place egg yolks and sugar in bowl over pan of steaming water and whisk for 5 minutes until thick and pale. Stir in passion fruit pulp and then fold in lightly whipped cream. Add 1 Crunchie bar (bashed with a rolling pin in bag), gently, so not to knock the air out. Pour into 4 moulds lined with cling film, and freeze. To serve, invert parfaits onto serving plates and remove cling film. Sprinkle the other Crunchie bar over the top.

# NECTARINE Platter served with a RASPBERRY Sorbet in the centre

(serves 6)

## INGREDIENTS
8 good nectarines, stoned and sliced, with skins on (white-flushed ones are the best)
1lb (450g) raspberries
2 x 1pt (500ml) raspberry sorbet (M&S, Tesco)
Few raspberries to garnish

### For raspberry coulis:
2lbs (1kg) raspberries
4oz (100g) caster sugar

## METHOD
Place sliced nectarines on pretty, flat, round or oval plate. Liquidise raspberries with sugar to make coulis. Sieve. To serve, place scoops of raspberry sorbet onto platter with nectarines then drizzle with coulis and add a few extra raspberries on top.

*Number one of my top ten to take to a desert island. Looks so pretty and summery, and is blissfully easy and unique.*

# PLUM & PORT Mousse

**(serves 6)**

*Superb when you have a glut of plums in the garden.*

## INGREDIENTS
1lb (450g) plums
4 heaped tablespoons granulated sugar
2 sherry glasses of port
4 sheets of leaf gelatine (soaked in bowl of cold water for 5 minutes then squeezed out)
3 eggs, separated
4oz (100g) caster sugar
½pt (300ml) double cream, lightly whipped

## METHOD
Put the plums and sugar in a saucepan and stew slowly. Remove stones when cool. Add port and whizz in liquidiser. This should make at least 6fl oz (150ml) of purée. Keep any extra to drizzle over mousse.

Heat a couple of tablespoons of plum purée and melt the gelatine into it until dissolved, then add to remainder of the plum and port purée. Beat egg yolks with the caster sugar until thick and creamy. Whip the egg whites in a separate bowl, to stiff peaks. Fold the plum and port purée into the egg yolk and sugar sabayon, followed by the whipped cream and lastly the egg whites. Carefully transfer into serving dish and chill in fridge for a couple of hours.

*This recipe was given to me by a great friend, Sue Leven, who is also a great cook.*

From quiet homes and first beginning
Out to the undiscovered ends.
There's nothing worth the wear of winning
But laughter and the love of friends

Hilaire Belloc

# RASPBERRY Soufflé with a White CHOCOLATE Sauce or RASPBERRY Coulis

(serves 4)

*This has the 'wow' factor.*

## INGREDIENTS

### For soufflé:
18oz (500g) raspberries plus a few extra raspberries for bottom of soufflés
5oz (125g) caster sugar
2½ tablespoons cornflour
4 teaspoons of cold water
1 vanilla pod
4 eggs, separated

### For white chocolate sauce:
4 tablespoons double cream
2oz (50g) white chocolate

### For raspberry coulis:
2lbs (1kg) raspberries
4ozs (100g) icing sugar

## METHOD

Lightly grease 4 ramekins with soft butter, sprinkle with a little caster sugar, then chill. Liquidise raspberries and blend until smooth. Add 4oz (100g) of caster sugar and whizz. Sieve into a large pan. Mix the cornflour and water together to form paste and set aside. Heat purée over medium heat and bring to boil, whisking all the time. Cut vanilla pod in half lengthways and scrape seeds into pan. Stir in the cornflour paste and continue to whisk until mixture starts to thicken. Remove from heat, leave to cool and chill for 20 minutes. Whisk egg whites with remaining caster sugar until thick, add to chilled purée and fold in well. Place a few raspberries in bottom of 4 ramekins. Divide the mixture into ramekins and bake in oven 400°F/200°C/Gas 6 for 10–12 minutes. Serve immediately with white chocolate sauce or raspberry coulis.

### For white chocolate sauce:
Place double cream and chocolate broken into bits in microwave bowl and microwave on medium for 45 seconds. Stir and microwave for another 30 seconds.

### For raspberry coulis:
Liquidise raspberries and icing sugar. Sieve.

**Clare's tip:**
*Ask guests to make a hole in the raspberry soufflés and pour in chocolate sauce.*

# STRAWBERRY Crème with a PRALINE Crunch

**(serves 6)**

*One that defeats my willpower.*

## INGREDIENTS
1lb (450g) sliced strawberries
8 egg yolks
1pt (600ml) double cream

### For praline crunch:
½lb (225g) flaked almonds
½lb (225g) caster sugar

## METHOD
Whisk egg yolks with 1 tablespoon cream. Boil rest of cream and pour over eggs. Pour into double saucepan and whisk over simmering water until it thickens. Meanwhile place a layer of strawberries at bottom of ramekins, cover with cooled cream mixture. Place in fridge to set. To make praline crunch, place sugar and almonds in heavy saucepan. Place pan over gentle heat and shake as sugar melts and turns to a deep golden brown. Pour mixture onto greased tin and leave to cool. Crack praline into small pieces with wooden spoon and sprinkle over cream mixture. Decorate with strawberry.

# Summer FRUIT Terrine

(serves 6-8)

## INGREDIENTS
600g fresh summer berries
(e.g. 200g raspberries, 200g
strawberries, 100g blueberries
and 100g blackberries)
1 bottle sparkling rosé wine
300g caster sugar
9 sheets leaf gelatine

## METHOD
Bring ⅓ of the bottle of wine to
boil with the sugar.

Soften the gelatine leaves in cold
water for 5 minutes, squeeze dry
and drop into the hot wine, stir
until dissolved. Add remaining
⅔ bottle of wine. Allow to stand
at room temperature so that it
remains liquid enough to pour.

Pour enough jelly into the base of
your mould or loaf tin to a depth
of about ½" (1cm).

Place the mould in a deep tray
with ice and water and into the
fridge to set.

Now place a layer of raspberries
over the layer of set jelly and pour
over some of the liquid jelly to
cover.

Return to fridge to set. Repeat
process with remaining fruit and
jelly. Refrigerate for several hours
before dipping mould into hot
water to help release the terrine.
Turn out onto a serving platter.

**Clare's tip:**
*If you plan to make the terrine a day in
advance you could use 1 less gelatine
leaf to prevent it becoming too rubbery.*

*Easy on the waistline.*

# ROSE Bavarois with Fresh RASPBERRIES

**(Serves 10)**

## INGREDIENTS
6 egg yolks
1pt (600ml) milk
4 teaspoons powdered gelatine (dissolved in 3 tablespoons hot water)
4oz (100g) caster sugar
1 tablespoon cornflour
¾pt (450ml) single cream
10 red rose petals + extra for decoration
1–2 tablespoons rose water
½pt (300ml) double cream

## METHOD
Beat egg yolks with sugar, cornflour and a little milk. Place rest of milk and single cream in pan and bring to the boil. Pour over egg yolk mixture, whisking constantly, then return to pan. Cook gently until thickened – do not boil. Strain custard into large bowl and stir in gelatine. Set bowl over iced water to cool mixture. Stir occasionally until beginning to set. Chop the rose petals finely and stir into cooked mixture with the rose water. Lightly whip double cream and fold into rose bavarois. Turn into shallow soufflé dish and chill for several hours. Unmould, decorate around the edge with fresh raspberries and sprinkle with extra red rose petals.

*Creamy, light and nourishing.*

THE ROSE

*The lily has a smooth stalk,*
*Will never hurt your hand;*
*But the rose upon her briar*
*Is lady of the land.*

*There's sweetness in*
*an apple tree,*
*And profit in the corn;*
*But the lady of all beauty*
*Is a rose upon a thorn.*

*When with moss and honey*
*She tips her bending briar,*
*And half unfolds her glowing*
*heart,*
*She sets the world on fire.*

Christina Rossetti

*Read at the christening*
*of my beloved grand-*
*daughter Rose*

# VANILLA Panna Cotta with a ROSÉ & RASPBERRY Jelly

**(serves 6)**

*An old faithful, number two on my list to take to my desert island.*

## INGREDIENTS

16fl oz (450ml) double cream
16fl oz (450ml) milk
1 vanilla pod
3oz (75g) caster sugar
5 gelatine leaves
Raspberries for decoration

**For raspberry coulis:**
2lbs (1kg) raspberries
4oz (100g) caster sugar

**For rosé jelly:**
2oz (50g) granulated sugar
4oz (100ml) rosé wine
1 leaf gelatine

## METHOD

**For raspberry coulis:**
Liquidise raspberries and caster sugar. Sieve.

**For rosé jelly:**
Place granulated sugar in pan with 4fl oz rosé wine. Warm gently until sugar dissolves. Soak gelatine in cold water for 5 minutes. Squeeze out excess water and stir into warm rosé wine until it dissolves. Divide between six pudding moulds, then drop 3–4 raspberries into bottom of each mould. Chill overnight to set.

**For panna cotta:**
Slit vanilla pod in half, scrape out seeds and place all in pan with cream, milk and sugar. Place over medium heat and bring slowly to boil. Remove from heat and set aside for ten minutes. Place 5 gelatine leaves in bowl of cold water to soak for five minutes. Bring cream back to boil, strain into bowl and discard vanilla pod. Drain gelatine leaves and squeeze out excess water. Add gelatine to hot cream and stir well to dissolve gelatine evenly. Cool. When just setting, pour over jelly. Chill for at least 4 hours until set. To serve, dip each mould briefly into hot water to loosen and turn out onto plates. Drizzle with raspberry coulis and serve with home-made shortbread.

# Warm CHOCOLATE Tart served with VANILLA Ice Cream or Clotted CREAM

(serves 4)

*To die for!*

## INGREDIENTS

4 x 4" (10cm) pastry cases (make or buy)

**For pastry:**
4oz (100g) flour
1oz (25g) sugar
2oz (50g) butter
½ beaten egg

**For tart filling:**
2oz (50g) double cream
6oz (150g) good dark chocolate
2 egg yolks
2oz (50g) sugar
2oz (50g) unsalted butter, diced
2 eggs
Vanilla ice-cream or clotted cream
4 teaspoons Dulce de Leche

## METHOD

For pastry, mix butter and flour until like breadcrumbs. Add sugar, then ½ beaten egg, and bind together. Rest in fridge for 20 minutes. Knead and roll thinly into 4 x 4" (10cm) pastry cases. Bake blind in oven 350°F/180°C/Gas 4 for 15 minutes. Cool and spread each tartlet with a teaspoon of Dulce de Leche

For tart filling, melt chocolate, cream and butter together in a bowl over pan of hot water. Whisk eggs and sugar together in another bowl over pan of hot water until pale and fluffy. Fold in chocolate mixture. Pour into tartlets and bake in oven 310°F/160°C/Gas 2/3 for 5 minutes until still soft in the middle. Serve warm with vanilla ice cream or clotted cream.

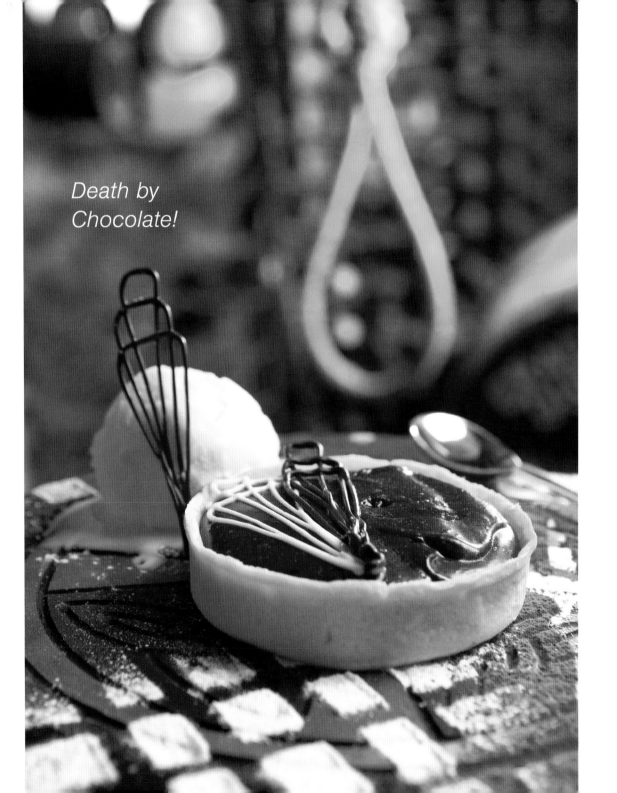

Death by
Chocolate!

# BLACKBERRY Jelly topped with a BLACKBERRY Fool

(serves 6-8)

*I have no willpower!*
*Another recipe I would*
*take to my desert island.*

## INGREDIENTS

**For blackberry fool:**
14oz (400g) blackberries + extra
for decoration
2 tablespoons icing sugar, sieved
1pt (400ml) double cream

**For blackberry jelly:**
12oz (300g) blackberries
1 leaf gelatine
2 tablespoons caster sugar

## METHOD

First make the jelly by placing blackberries in pan with caster sugar. Soften gently and sieve. Measure liquid and dissolve 1 leaf of gelatine for ¼pt (150ml) of blackberry juice. Cool and pour into bottom of pretty glasses. Leave to set. Meanwhile make the blackberry fool. Place the blackberries and sugar in saucepan with 2 tablespoons water and cook over low heat for 5–10 minutes until soft. Mash in bowl with a potato masher. Leave to cool. Whip cream, then fold in blackberries. Chill for 30 minutes.

Spoon blackberry fool over jelly and decorate with a blackberry. Serve with lemon shortbread.

# RASPBERRY & White CHOCOLATE Terrine

(serves 8)

## INGREDIENTS

**For raspberry ice cream:**
1pt (600ml) double cream
1 large tin condensed milk
1lb (450g) raspberries
½lb (225g) raspberries for decoration

**For coulis (liquidised):**
1lb (450g) raspberries
2 tablespoons of caster sugar
Sugar to taste

**For chocolate filling:**
6oz (150g) white chocolate
6 tablespoons (120ml) single cream

## METHOD

Whip double cream and condensed milk until thick. Fold in 1lb (450g) raspberries (liquidised and sieved). Freeze half ice cream in 2lb (900g) loaf tin, lined with cling film, until firm to touch. Melt white chocolate and cream gently in pan. Cool a little and spread over top of raspberry ice cream.

Freeze for 20 minutes. Then spread rest of ice cream on top, cover with foil and freeze for several hours. To serve, turn out (it may be necessary to dip base of tin in warm water) onto flat plate. Slice and place 2 pieces of terrine on individual plates, sprinkle with raspberries and drizzle with raspberry coulis.

*A great favourite.*

Fantastic to have in the deep
freeze, lovely for summer.

Winter
at Ballindalloch

# White CHOCOLATE Mousse in a CHOCOLATE Cup drizzled with a PASSION FRUIT Coulis

**(serves 4-6)**

## INGREDIENTS
9oz (250g) white chocolate, broken into pieces
2½fl oz (60ml) milk
1 vanilla pod, split and seeds scraped out
3 free range eggs, separated
½pt (300ml) whipping cream, whipped
4 passion fruit, halved and seeds scooped out (optional)
4–6 chocolate cups (make or buy)

## METHOD
Put the chocolate and milk in a heatproof bowl placed over a pan of gently simmering water. Heat until the chocolate is just melted, stirring regularly. Stir in the vanilla seeds, then leave to cool for 5 minutes. Add the egg yolks, one at a time, beating well between each addition. Fold in the whipped cream. Whisk the egg whites until they form soft peaks, then fold half into the chocolate mixture, followed by the remaining half.

Divide the mousse between 6 chocolate cups. Leave to set. To serve, swirl passion fruit pulp over top of each cup.

**Clare's tip:**
*Can be served in a sundae glass drizzled with passion fruit coulis.*

*A choc-o-holic's dream.*

# BANANA Parfait Bonnie Prince Charlie

(serves 4-6)

## INGREDIENTS
3 bananas
6 egg yolks
4oz (125g) icing sugar
2 tablespoons Drambuie or
banana liqueur (warmed)
½pt double cream
(whipped, soft peak)
Juice of 1 lemon
Caramelised banana (to garnish)

So easy, so elegant

## METHOD
Whisk the yolks, icing sugar and warmed liqueur until thick. Process peeled bananas in a blender with the lemon juice, and add to the whisked egg yolk mixture. Fold in the lightly whipped cream. Transfer the parfait mix into 8 individual moulds, and freeze for several hours until firm.

When ready to serve cut some slices of banana on the diagonal, Dip into a little sugar and place in a very hot Teflon coated pan. The banana will quickly caramelise. Lift onto plate.

Dip the parfaits briefly in hot water to help unmould them onto serving plates and pour chocolate sauce over the parfait or use some warmed Dulce de Leche.

Clare's tip:
*Delicious with chocolate sauce:*

*4oz (100g) good dark chocolate*
*4 tablespoons (120ml) single cream*

*Melt in pan together and serve.*

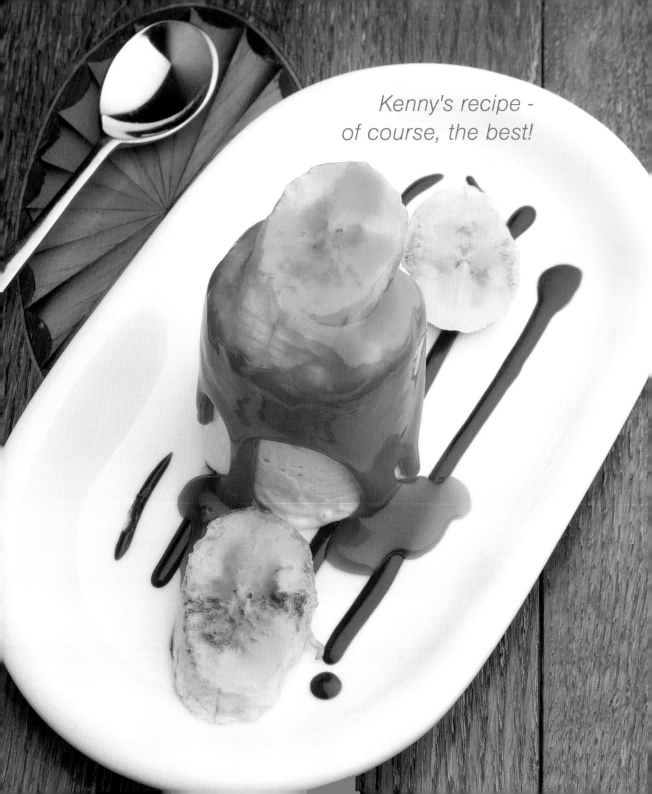

*Kenny's recipe -
of course, the best!*

# Teatime

According to legend, one of Queen Victoria's (1819–1901) ladies-in-waiting, Anna Maria Stanhope (1783–1857) - one of my husband Oliver's ancestors - known as the Duchess of Bedford, is credited as the creator of afternoon teatime. Because the noon meal had become skimpier, the Duchess suffered from "a sinking feeling" at about 4 o'clock in the afternoon.

At first the Duchess had her servants sneak her a pot of tea and a few breadstuffs. Adopting the European tea service format, she invited friends to join her for an additional afternoon meal at five o'clock in her rooms at Belvoir Castle. The menu centred around small cakes, bread and butter, sandwiches, assorted sweets, and of course, tea. This summer practice proved so popular, the Duchess continued it when she returned to London, sending cards to her friends asking them to join her for "tea and a walking the fields." The practice of inviting friends to come for tea in the afternoon was quickly picked up by other social hostesses.

I adore tea and definitely, like the Duchess, suffer from a sinking feeling at about 4 o'clock! In those days, the menu centred around small cakes and sweets, which I think is an excellent idea, so I have concentrated on traybakes, which are practical and long-lasting. Although the afternoon tea ritual has fallen somewhat out of favour in recent times, here at Ballindalloch Castle it is one of the fine old traditions which we like to maintain.

Royal Teatime
A very special slice of cake

# Mrs D's Scottish Brown BREAD

## INGREDIENTS
4oz (100g) self-raising flour
8oz (225g) wholemeal flour or
granary flour
1 small teaspoon bicarbonate of
soda
1 small teaspoon cream of tartar
1 small teaspoon sugar
½pt (300ml) buttermilk
A pinch of salt

## METHOD
Mix dry ingredients together. Add
buttermilk and mix well. Pour into
loaf tin, cover with foil and bake at
375°F/190°C/Gas 5 for 35
minutes. Remove foil and bake for
further 5 minutes.

**Clare's tip:**
*Delicious if you add 3oz (75g)*
*chopped walnuts, pecans, almonds,*
*cheese or herbs*

## Ballindalloch ORANGE SHORTBREAD dipped in ORANGE CHOCOLATE

### INGREDIENTS
8oz (200g) plain flour
4oz (100g) cornflour
4oz (100g) icing sugar
8oz (200g) butter
Zest of 1 orange
6oz (150g) dark orange chocolate

### METHOD
Chop butter into small pieces and place into processor with sieved flour, cornflour, grated zest of orange and icing sugar. Whizz until it gathers into a ball. Turn out onto floured surface and roll out to ¼" (½cm) thick. Cut into rounds with pastry cutter and place on greased baking tray. Cook for 15–20 minutes at 350ºF/180ºC/Gas 4 until firm and light brown. Place on wire rack. Cool. Meanwhile melt dark orange chocolate in microwave then dip shortbread half into chocolate and place on parchment paper on baking tray to harden.

## Ballindalloch LEMON SHORTBREAD dipped in WHITE CHOCOLATE

### INGREDIENTS
8oz (200g) plain flour
4oz (100g) cornflour
4oz (100g) icing sugar
8oz (200g) butter
Zest of 1 lemon
6oz (150g) white chocolate

### METHOD
Chop butter into small pieces and place into processor with sieved flour, cornflour, grated zest of lemon and icing sugar. Whizz until it gathers into a ball. Turn out onto floured surface and roll out to ¼" (½cm) thick. Cut into rounds with pastry cutter and place on greased baking tray. Cook for 15–20 minutes at 350ºF/180ºC/Gas 4 until firm and light brown. Place on wire rack. Cool. Meanwhile, melt white chocolate in microwave then dip shortbread half into chocolate and place on parchment paper on baking tray to harden.

*Scottish shortbread with an orange and lemon twist!*

# Millionaire's White CHOCOLATE Shortbread with HAZELNUTS and RAISINS

## INGREDIENTS

**For shortbread:**
2oz (50g) butter
1oz (25g) caster sugar
3oz (75g) plain flour

**For toffee:**
4oz (100g) butter
2oz (50g) caster sugar
2 tablespoons golden syrup
½ tin (7oz/200g) sweetened condensed milk
Few drops vanilla essence
3oz (75g) raisins
3oz (75g) whole hazelnuts

**For topping:**
8oz (200g) good white chocolate

## METHOD

**For base:**
Rub flour, butter and sugar together until mixture resembles fine bread crumbs. Press into tin 8" x 12" (20cm x 30cm). Bake at 325ºF/160ºC/Gas 3 for approximately 20 minutes until light brown. Leave to cool.

**For toffee and topping:**
Melt all toffee ingredients (not raisins or hazelnuts) in pan and boil for 5 minutes stirring continually. Cool a little. Sprinkle raisins and hazelnuts over shortbread, then pour toffee over top. Cool. Melt chocolate in bowl over pan of boiling water and spread on top of toffee. When set and cool, cut into squares.

*I could eat these all day long!*

# CHOCOLATE & CARAMEL Cake

## INGREDIENTS

6oz (150g) self-raising flour
2 large tablespoons cocoa powder
1 teaspoon bicarbonate of soda
5oz (125g) caster sugar
¼pt (150ml) corn oil
¼pt (150ml) milk
2 eggs
2 teaspoons vanilla essence
1 x 14oz (397g) can Carnation caramel/Dulce de Leche
4oz (100g) good dark chocolate (70% cocoa) broken into pieces
1 tablespoon icing sugar
Chocolate flake or strawberries for decoration

## METHOD

Sieve flour, cocoa powder and bicarbonate of soda into large mixing bowl and stir in caster sugar. Pour corn oil and milk into measuring jug, add eggs and 1 teaspoon vanilla essence and whisk lightly to mix. Beat 2 tablespoons of Carnation caramel/Dulce de Leche in bowl until smooth, then whisk into egg and oil mixture. Add wet ingredients with dry and mix well.

Pour mixture into 2 x 7" (18cm) sandwich tins (bottom lined with baking parchment) and bake at 350°F/180°C/Gas 4 for 20–25 minutes until cake is springy to touch. Leave to cool in tin, then turn onto wire rack and peel off baking parchment. Melt pieces of chocolate in bowl over simmering water, stirring until smooth. Add remaining Carnation caramel/Dulce de Leche and vanilla essence and beat well until glossy. Sieve in icing sugar and mix thoroughly. Place one cake upside down on a plate, spread with some of the icing then top with other half of cake. Spread the entire cake with rest of icing. Sprinkle with crushed chocolate flake or decorate with chocolate flowers.

*Happiness is an elasticated waist.*

# Baby BANOFFEE Tartlets

(serves 4)

*A big cheat but wonderful when you are stressed out! Can be used for tea or pudding.*

## INGREDIENTS
8 tartlet cases (buy from M&S)
2 jars Dulce de Leche (caramel)
2 ripe bananas, sliced
¼pt (150ml) double cream, chilled
1 dessertspoon icing sugar
1 Cadbury's chocolate flake

## METHOD
Spoon Dulce de Leche into tartlets, halfway. Crush bananas and icing sugar with a fork and fold in whipped cream. Pour on top of caramel, and sprinkle with chocolate flake. Delicious served with vanilla ice-cream.

# CHOCOLATE Nutty Cookies

(serves 6-8)

## INGREDIENTS
3oz (75g) butter
3oz (75g) granulated sugar
3oz (75g) light muscovado sugar
1 egg
6oz (175g) self raising flour
1 bar Toblerone (100g), roughly chopped

## METHOD
Cream together butter and sugar in bowl until light and fluffy. Then beat in egg. Fold in flour and Toblerone pieces. Place large teaspoonfuls of mixture onto lightly greased baking trays, spacing well apart to allow mixture to spread. Bake at 350°F/180°C/ Gas 4 for 12–15 minutes. Remove from oven and cool on baking trays for 2–3 minutes. Then transfer to wire rack to finish cooling.

## Mars Bar & CHOCOLATE Flake Crispy Traybake

(serves 6-8)

*Children's favourite.*

### INGREDIENTS
1 chocolate flake
2 large Mars bars (+ extra Mars bar for decoration)
1 tablespoon golden syrup
2oz (50g) butter
6oz (150g) rice crispies
12oz (350g) milk chocolate to cover

### METHOD
Melt 2 Mars bars, syrup and butter in large bowl in microwave. Add rice crispies. Press into 9" x 12" (23cm x 30cm) baking tray lined with greaseproof paper. Cool in fridge. Spread with melted chocolate. Decorate with slices of Mars bar and small chunks of chocolate flake.

## Mrs D's Mouthwatering GINGERBREAD

(serves 4)

### INGREDIENTS
8oz (225g) plain flour
4oz (100g) margarine
6fl oz (175ml) black treacle
2oz (50g) golden syrup
2oz (50g) granulated sugar
¼pt (150ml) milk
1 teaspoon baking soda
1 teaspoon mixed spice
1 teaspoon ground ginger
2 eggs beaten

### METHOD
Melt margarine, syrup and treacle in pan Add ¼pt (150ml) milk. Cool. Add beaten eggs. Mix dry ingredients together and add to pan. Line loaf tin with non-stick baking paper and bake at 325°F/160°C/Gas 3 for 1¼ - 1½ hours.

# Nanny Sandra's GINGER Crunch

**(serves 4)**

## INGREDIENTS
8oz (225g) plain flour
3½oz (100g) caster sugar
1 teaspoon baking powder
2 teaspoons ground ginger
5½oz (150g) butter,
cut into cubes

### For icing:
5½oz (150g) butter
4 tablespoons (60ml) golden syrup
10½oz (300g) icing sugar, sifted
2 tablespoons ground ginger

## METHOD
To make the base, put the flour, sugar, baking powder and ginger in a food processor. Pulse several times to combine, then add the butter. Process for about 30 seconds, or until the mixture resembles fine breadcrumbs (this can also be done by hand). Press the mixture evenly into a tin 8" x 12" (21cm x 30cm) lined with cooking parchment. Bake in oven 350°F/180°C/Gas 4 for 20–25 minutes or until lightly golden.

Remove from the oven and allow to cool completely. To make the icing, put the butter and golden syrup in a medium saucepan and heat until just melted. Add the sifted icing sugar and ginger and cook for a further 1 to 2 minutes, stirring constantly until smooth. Remove from the heat and pour over the base. Leave to set. Remove from the tin and cut into squares or triangles to serve.

194

## BREAD-AND-BUTTER PUDDING

Ingredients:
1 egg
2 teaspoonfuls of castor sugar (these are for the custard)
6 thin slices of bread-and-butter

1 breakfastcupful of milk
A few sultanas or raisins (or mixed peel)
Grated lemon rind
Demerara sugar
A small nut of butter

*Method.*—Butter a small shallow pie-dish, and line it with slices of buttered bread. Sprinkle with Demerara sugar and sultanas or raisins, and discreetly grate the rind of a lemon. Fill up with custard (see p. 46), and bake slowly. When this has set place thin slices of bread-and-butter on top, and sprinkle with sultanas or raisins and Demerara sugar. Bake slowly in a moderate oven for about fifteen minutes, and then brown slightly under the grill, if necessary. Serve very hot, or iced, with whipped cream.

Time about 40 minutes.

Sufficient for 2 persons.

A more solid pudding may be obtained by filling the pie-dish with thin slices of bread-and-butter, the dried fruit, and sugar, and pouring in the liquid custard until the top of the dish is reached. Bake in a fairly warm oven.

## SWEET CARROT PUDDING

Ingredients
1 lb. of carrots
Half their bulk in bread-crumbs
1 egg

2 oz. of butter
1 oz. of Demerara sugar
Lemon sauce (see p. 50)
Salt

*Method.*—Scrub the carrots, put them into boiling water, and cook until soft. Rub them through a sieve. Add the bread-crumbs, sugar, butter, a pinch of salt, and sufficient egg to bind well together. (A little flour and milk may be used instead of egg if desired.) Butter a pudding-basin, put in the mixture, steam for three-quarters of an hour to set. Turn out, Pudding, and serve hot with lemon sauce.

Time about 1½ hours.

Sufficient for 4 persons.

## CASTLE PUDDING

... are the same as for standard pound-cake mixture (see p. 238). Beat the butter and sugar to a cream, add the egg then stir in the flour and baking-powder. Put the mixture into cast-method may be added, if liked. Put the mixture into cast-ing tins, and bake or steam as desired. The puddings may be baked and turned out a little hole in the top of ally served thus: Scoop out a little hole in the top of coconut, custard, or jelly, etc., and serve with a fruit sauce. Fill with jam, ptake about 30 minutes if baked, about 45 minutes if s

Sufficient for 4 persons.

*Variation.*—Fill the top with whipped cream, and ser hot chocolate sauce with the puddings.

## STEAMED DATE PUDDING

Ingredients
2 oz. of suet
2 oz. of breadcrumbs
1 tablespoonful of golden syrup
½ teaspoonful of nutmeg

6 oz. of dates
1 oz. of flour
¼ gill of milk
1 egg

*Method.*—Stone the dates, chop the suet, and rub both into the breadcrumbs and flour. Dissolve the syrup in the milk over a gentle heat, add the egg and nutmeg, and pour into the dry in-gredients. Mix all well together, and put into a greased basin. Cover with greaseproof paper and steam for an hour.

Time about 1½ hours.

Sufficient for 3 persons.

## DUMPLINGS

Ingredients
1 lb. of self-raising flour
2 to 4 oz. of suet
A pinch of salt

1 teacupful of water
A few breadcrumbs, if

*Method.*—Mix the flour and chopped suet together wi of salt. Stir into a stiff paste with the water. Divid into small round balls, and throw them into boiling w Do not make the mistake of making the dumplings too have many and small than large and few. Th

# WHISKY & RAISIN
# Traybake

## INGREDIENTS
5oz (125g) seedless raisins
6 eggs (separated)
¼pt (150ml) Ballindalloch Whisky
4oz (100g) plain flour
6oz (150g) ground almonds
14oz (400g) good dark cooking chocolate
8oz (225g) unsalted butter
4fl oz (100ml) warm water
8oz (225g) sugar

### For chocolate and honey icing:
8oz (225g) good dark cooking chocolate
4oz (100g) unsalted butter
2 tablespoons clear honey
1 chocolate flake or packet of Maltesers

## METHOD
Soak raisins in whisky overnight. Sieve flour into bowl, add almonds and mix. Melt butter and chocolate in bowl placed over pan of simmering water. Stir until smooth. Add warm water. Beat egg yolks and sugar until pale and thick. Add melted chocolate and mix well. Fold in flour and almonds. Then add whisky and raisins. Whisk egg whites to soft peaks. Add tablespoon of egg whites to chocolate mixture, then fold in rest. Pour into tin 8¾" (22cm) square, lined with greaseproof paper. Bake in oven 350°F/180°C/Gas 4 for about 45 minutes. Cool. Meanwhile, make icing. Place all ingredients in bowl and melt over pan of simmering water, stirring until smooth. Remove cake from tin and spread with icing. Sprinkle with crushed chocolate flake or Maltesers.

*A recipe from the brilliant Australian cook Stephanie Alexandra.*

# St Clement's Traybake

## INGREDIENTS
7oz (200g) plain flour
2 teaspoons baking powder
7oz (200g) caster sugar
4 eggs
¼pt (150ml) soured cream
Grated rind of 1 large lemon
4 tablespoons lemon juice
¼pt (150ml) sunflower oil

### For syrup:
4 tablespoons icing sugar
3 tablespoons lemon juice

### For icing:
8oz (225g) fondant icing sugar
Finely grated rind and juice of ½ orange
2 tablespoons lemon juice

## METHOD
Grease and line a baking tin 8½" x 12" (22cm x 30cm). Sieve flour and baking powder and mix in sugar. Whisk (or blend in food processor) eggs, soured cream, lemon rind and juice and oil. Add dry ingredients and mix well. Pour mixture into the prepared tin and bake in pre-heated oven 350°F/180°C/Gas 4 for about 25–30 minutes until risen and golden.

To make syrup, stir lemon juice and icing sugar in pan over low heat until just beginning to bubble and turn syrupy. Brush the syrup over the top of the sponge as soon as it comes out of the oven.

To make the icing, mix the lemon and orange juices and orange rind with the sifted fondant icing sugar in pan to the consistency of pouring cream. Warm through on low heat to a temperature which would feel uncomfortably hot to the hand. Pour immediately over the soaked sponge and allow to set. Make up a little extra icing, add colour, and pipe lines across traybake. Leave the traybake to cool completely in the tin. When set, cut into squares.

# Supper Time

# Crêpes GRUYÈRE

(serves 4)

## INGREDIENTS

**For crêpes (make or buy):**
1oz (30g) plain flour
2½fl oz (75ml) milk
1 egg
½ tablespoon chopped mixed herbs (parsley, chive & dill)
Salt and pepper

**For béchamel sauce:**
1oz (25g) flour
1oz (25g) butter
¾pt (425ml) milk

**To finish:**
4oz (120g) cooked prawns
3oz (90g) Gruyère
2oz (60g) red Cheddar

## METHOD

**First make the crêpes:**
Sieve flour, make a well, add egg, a little milk and salt and pepper and mix to a smooth batter. Add remainder of milk. Cover and rest for 20–30 minutes before stirring through the herbs. Cook 4 crêpes over a high heat in a non stick frying pan greased with a little butter, for around 30 seconds on each side. Use just enough batter to cover the base of the frying pan.

**For béchamel sauce:**
Melt butter and add flour and cook out for several minutes. Add milk all at once and whisk until it thickens over a medium heat, for a few minutes.

Add prawns and salt and pepper and spread onto crêpes then fold into quarters. Place the 4 crêpes onto a roasting dish and top with grated cheese. Bake in a hot oven for 5–10 minutes until hot and crispy.

# Creamy SMOKED SALMON & PRAWN Risotto

(serves 4)

## INGREDIENTS

2 tablespoons olive oil
1 small onion, finely chopped
6oz (150g) risotto rice
3½fl oz (100ml) white wine
1pt (600ml) hot vegetable stock
2oz (50g) Philadelphia cream
cheese with chives (light)
3oz (75g) smoked salmon, sliced
into strips
2oz (50g) large prawns
1 tablespoon chopped dill for
garnish

## METHOD

Heat olive oil in deep frying pan,
add onion and cook until soft. Stir
in rice and cook for one minute
until rice grains are coated with
oil. Pour over wine and allow to
evaporate. Add 3½fl oz (100ml) of
stock to pan, stir occasionally and
cook over gentle heat for about
15 minutes, adding more stock
when needed. Stir in Philadelphia,
smoked salmon and prawns until
warm. Spoon into serving dish
and sprinkle with dill. Serve with a
green salad.

*Delicious!*
*The best risotto ever!*

# Hot SMOKED SALMON Kedgeree

**(serves 4)**

Always a favourite and heats up well with a little extra butter.

## INGREDIENTS

12oz (350g) brown Basmati rice
12oz (350g) hot smoked salmon, skinned and flaked
1 tablespoon vegetable oil
1 large onion, finely chopped
12 green cardamom pods, split open
¼ teaspoon turmeric
4" (10cm) cinnamon stick
3 bay leaves
1pt (600ml) chicken stock
3 tablespoons chopped fresh parsley
1 teaspoon white wine vinegar
4 eggs

## METHOD

Cover rice with water and leave to soak for 10 minutes. Meanwhile, heat oil in large saucepan. Add onion and cook gently for 5 minutes until opaque. Add cardamom, turmeric, cinnamon and bay leaves. Cook for minute. Drain rice, and add to the saucepan, stirring well. Add stock and a little salt and pepper, bring to boil and stir. Cover with a lid and cook gently for about 30 minutes. Uncover rice, remove bay leaves, cinnamon and cardamom pods. Gently fold in hot smoked salmon, cover again and cook slowly on low heat for about 5 minutes until fish is heated through. Stir in parsley and season to taste. Keep warm. Meanwhile, poach eggs in boiling water with a teaspoon of vinegar. Take out gently with slotted spoon and top each plate of kedgeree with a poached egg.

# Warm Poached EGGS on SMOKED SALMON topped with AVOCADO & PRAWN Mayonnaise

**(serves 4)**

## INGREDIENTS
4 rounds of fried bread
4 eggs
1 avocado pear, peeled, stoned and halved
4 tablespoons Hellman's mayonnaise
Juice and zest of ½ lemon
4oz (100g) small cooked prawns
4 slices smoked salmon
Salt and pepper
Parsley for decoration (finely chopped)

## METHOD
Fry rounds of bread in oil. Pat with kitchen paper to take off excess fat. Keep warm. Poach eggs lightly and keep warm. Whizz avocado, juice and zest of lemon, salt and pepper and mayonnaise in processor until thick and creamy. Fold prawns into avocado mayonnaise. Place fried bread on individual plates. Cover with smoked salmon slice and top with poached egg. Pour avocado mixture gently over top and sprinkle with parsley.

Perfect for a summer supper.

# CHICKEN LIVER Croustades

(serves 4)

## INGREDIENTS

4 slices brown or
wholemeal bread
½oz (15g) butter (soft)
8oz (225g) chicken livers,
trimmed, rinsed and dried
1 teaspoon grainy mustard
2 teaspoons flour
3 teaspoons brandy or sherry
4 slices streaky bacon (grilled and
chopped)
¼pt single cream
Salt and pepper

## METHOD

Mix butter with mustard. Roll
bread with rolling pin to flatten.
Trim crusts and spread with half
the mustard mixture. Gently press
bread into deep, greased patty
tins with mustard side uppermost.
Bake at 400°F/200°C/Gas 6
for about 15 minutes. Heat in
frying pan remaining mustard
mixture and add chicken livers.
Cook gently, sauté for about
2–3 minutes. Sprinkle flour on to
livers. Pour in brandy then cream.
Simmer for 2–3 minutes until
sauce thickens. Season. Place
warm croustades on individual
plates and fill with chicken liver
mixture. Sprinkle with grilled
bacon surrounded with rocket
leaves or parsley.

Chicken livers are back in
fashion, they are not only
delicious but inexpensive.

# Woof!

### recipes for our
### best friends

## RABBIT Ragout
### - adored by cats AND dogs!

*Let's catch the rabbit first!*

### INGREDIENTS

1 rabbit (skinned & jointed)
1 onion (peeled & halved)
1 carrot

### METHOD

Heat one tablespoon of oil in a pan. Add rabbit pieces and brown all over. Add onion and carrot and enough water to cover. Bring to simmer and cook in a covered pan for one to two hours until meat falls off the bone. Cool and shred.

## CHICKEN Broth Bone

### INGREDIENTS

3 cups white flour
¾ cup yellow cornmeal
1 cup chicken stock
4 tablespoons softened margarine
1 egg
1 tablespoon milk

### METHOD

Combine flour, cornmeal, chicken stock and margarine. Knead dough for a few minutes. Sprinkle worktop and rolling pin with flour and roll out dough to ¼" (6mm) thick. Cut out biscuits with animal cookie cutter. Beat egg and milk together and brush over top of biscuits. Bake at 350°F/180°C/ Gas 4 for about 30 minutes on a non-greased baking tray.

*Sausage dog!*

# PEANUT BUTTER Bone

Definitely a doggie bone with a 5-paw rating!

## INGREDIENTS

2 tablespoons corn oil
½ cup peanut butter
1 cup water
1 cup wholewheat flour
2 cups white flour

## METHOD

Combine oil, peanut butter and water. Add flour, one cup at a time and knead into firm dough. Roll dough out to ¼" (6mm) thickness, then cut out shapes with animal cookie cutter. Place on a baking tray and bake at 350°F/180°C/Gas 4 for about 20 minutes.

# PHEASANT or TURKEY Sausage

## INGREDIENTS

Minced pheasant breasts, or turkey
Low sodium breadcrumbs
Parmesan cheese
Parsley

## METHOD

Place minced meat in large mixing bowl. Add 1 teaspoon of parsley per 1lb (450g) of meat and 1 tablespoon of Parmesan cheese per 1lb (450g) of meat. Stir in breadcrumbs until mixture is a little dry. Then roll mixture into balls, without it sticking to your hands (too moist) or crumbling (too dry). Adjust accordingly. Place on tray lined with baking parchment. Bake at 350°F/180°C/Gas 4 until golden brown and cooked inside. Tip onto kitchen roll to remove excess grease. Cool and store in freezer or eat* within a few days.

* instruction to dog, not to the cook!

Miaow!
recipes
for the boss

SIGNED COPY

138 ravishing recipes from the
Lady Laird of Ballindalloch Castle

ENSE ET ANIMO

TOUCH NOT THE CAT BOT A GLOVE

**As all cat-lovers know well,
cats understand human language, they simply choose to
ignore it most of the time - but they do learn exceptionally
quickly when there is a rattle in the tin!**

## Cat Cookies

### INGREDIENTS
½ cup wheatgerm
½ cup dry milk
1 teaspoon honey
1 small jar beef purée baby food

### METHOD
Mix together wheatgerm, dry milk and honey in bowl. Add beef purée and stir until thoroughly mixed. Form into balls (size of marbles), place on greased tray and flatten with fork. Bake at 350°F/180°C/Gas 4 for about 8–10 minutes. Cool and store in airtight tin in fridge.

## MACKEREL Munchies

### INGREDIENTS
½ cup tinned mackerel, drained
1 egg, beaten
1 cup breadcrumbs
1 teaspoon brewers' yeast

### METHOD
Place all ingredients in bowl. Mix with fork. Form mixture into balls (size of marbles) and place on greased tray. Bake at 350°F/180°C/Gas 4 for 6–8 minutes until golden and crispy. Cool and store in airtight tin in fridge.

**Tweet**
up before the beak...

# Bird Cake

*This is easy to buy but more fun to make - especially if you live in the depths of the country!*

## INGREDIENTS
One third lard/fat
Two thirds oatmeal
Cheese
Seeds
Nuts
Dried fruit

## METHOD
Melt lard/fat and mix together the dry ingredients. Place in container or half a coconut shell to set. Place near or on your bird table or hang as in photo.

Ray Kennedy (rspb-images.com)

# Nibble
## the Red Squirrels of Ballindalloch Castle

## Red Squirrel Menu

Hazelnuts in shell
Peanuts in shells (monkey nuts)
Peanut kernels
Pine nuts
Walnuts in shells
You need a blank cheque! They are
seriously high maintenance, but worth it!

# TOP TIPS for FLORAL arrangements

**Flowers always seem to go with food and romance, and as a former pupil of the late Constance Spry I thought I might add a few tips for arranging flowers for your dinner table. Flowers are like most things in life, they change with fashion. In the old days you had to spend hours wiring and measuring. Today the fashion is what I call 'plonk' vases – just buy the made-up bunches at the supermarket and 'plonk' them in! But it really is worth the effort to do them yourself.**

**1.** First, choose flowers, scented ones if possible, to complement your colour scheme.

**2.** Remember to arrange flowers so that you can talk over the top of them!

**3.** Also remember the Constance Spry tip to work on a measurement of one-third vase to two-thirds flowers.

**4.** Always use a mixture of flower shapes, tall spiky ones, medium-sized flowers of all shapes, and round pudgy ones to go in the middle.

**5.** Always use odd numbers of flowers and group varieties together.

**6.** Use wild flowers as well as bought ones. They are always beautiful and natural, like God's garden.

**7.** Remember to start with foliage to give shape to your arrangements.

**8.** If you are having a special dinner, it is lovely to complement it with a single flower placed on the napkin.

**9.** Another fun thing to do which is very effective is to put lots of little vases of different shapes down the centre of the table, or in the middle in a circle.

**10.** My most perfect arrangements are bowls of the same flower which have a scent. There is nothing more lovely than vases of roses, sweet peas, hyacinths or lily-of-the-valley.

# SMOOTHIES & drinks

*Non-alcohlic tipples (fruit whizzes). I have fallen in love with smoothies. They are healthy, easy to make and easy on the waistline. Here are one or two of my favourites and one or two other liquid delights...*

## Gold TROPICAL Smoothie

(serves 2-4)

### INGREDIENTS
2 ripe passion fruit
1 large ripe mango, peeled and cut into chunks
1 small ripe pineapple, peeled and chopped
1 large banana, peeled and chopped
14ozs (400g) natural yogurt
Handful of ice cubes

### METHOD
Scoop out pulp from passion fruit into liquidiser (sieve if you don't like the seeds). Add all ingredients and whizz. Pour into glasses and enjoy straight away.

## BERRY Smoothie

(serves 2)

### INGREDIENTS
12ozs (350g) frozen mixed berries
8fl ozs (250ml) cranberry juice
2 frozen bananas
2 tablespoons natural yogurt
Handful of crushed ice
A few berries to garnish

### METHOD
Place all ingredients in liquidiser and whizz until smooth. Pour into glasses and sprinkle with berries.

## Clare's LEMONADE

(serves 2)

### INGREDIENTS
1pt (600ml) water
2 tablespoons caster sugar
2 large lemons
(washed well)

### METHOD
Cut lemons into quarters and de-pip. Place in liquidiser, add water and sugar. Whizz to slow count of ten. Sieve and chill.

# PEAR Smoothie

(serves 2)

## INGREDIENTS
8fl ozs (250ml) natural yogurt
2 Comice pears, peeled,
cored and diced
2 kiwi fruits, peeled and sliced
Handful of ice cubes
Mint leaves for garnish

## METHOD
Place all ingredients in liquidiser
and whizz until smooth. Pour into
glasses and garnish with mint
leaves.

# Pink Fizz

(serves 4-6)

For kids, drivers and slimmers.

## INGREDIENTS
1¾pts (1litre) cranberry juice
1¾pts (1litre) apple juice
1¾pts (1litre) sparkling water
Punnet cranberries and apple slices

## METHOD
Mix juices together and place
in fridge to chill. Mix before
serving, then sprinkle with fresh
cranberries and apple slices in
large jug.

# Hot Toddy

(serves 1)

A great remedy for coughs and
colds - also a wonderful warmer.

## INGREDIENTS
2 slices lemon for garnish
4 cloves
2fl ozs (50ml) whisky
1fl oz (25ml) freshly-squeezed
lemon juice
2–3 teaspoons runny honey
3fl ozs (75ml) hot water
1 cinnamon stick

## METHOD
Stick cloves into lemon slices. Mix
all remaining ingredients in jug.
Pour into tall heatproof glass and
top with lemon slices.

# Weights and Measures

- but the scales always lie!

## OVEN TEMPERATURE CHART

| °C | °F | Gas Mark |
|---|---|---|
| 110 | 225 | ¼ |
| 130 | 250 | ½ |
| 140 | 275 | 1 |
| 150 | 300 | 2 |
| 170 | 325 | 3 |
| 180 | 350 | 4 |
| 190 | 375 | 5 |
| 200 | 400 | 6 |
| 220 | 425 | 7 |
| 230 | 450 | 8 |
| 240 | 475 | 9 |

## SPOON MEASUREMENTS

| | |
|---|---|
| 1 teaspoon | 5 mls |
| 4 teaspoons approximately | 1 tablespoon |
| 1 tablespoon approximately | 20 mls |
| 1 rounded spoon | 2 level spoons |

## METRIC CONVERSION SCALE

| LIQUID | | | SOLID | | |
|---|---|---|---|---|---|
| Imperial | Exact Conversion | Recommended ml | Imperial | Exact Conversion | Recommended g |
| ¼ pint | 142 ml | 150 ml | 1 oz | 28.35 g | 25 g |
| ½ pint | 284 ml | 300 ml | 2 oz | 56.7 g | 50 g |
| 1 pint | 568 ml | 600 ml | 4 oz | 113.4 g | 100 g |
| 1½ pints | 851 ml | 900 ml | 8 oz | 226.8 g | 225 g |
| 1¾ pints | 992 ml | 1 litre | 12 oz | 340.2 g | 350 g |
| | | | 14 oz | 397.0 g | 400 g |
| | | | 16 oz (1 lb) | 453.6 g | 450 g |
| | | | 2.2 lb | 1 kilogram(kg) | |

Leaf gelatine

soak in ice cold water

until softened

squeeze out & dissolve into hot liquid

# AMERICAN CONVERSION OF WEIGHTS AND MEASURES

(Note: UK ounces and metric grams are weighed)

| | US Standard | UK | Metric |
|---|---|---|---|
| Flour | ¼ cup | 1 oz | 25 g |
| | ½ cup | 2 oz | 50 g |
| | ¾ cup | 3 oz | 75 g |
| | 1 cup | 4 oz | 100 g |
| Icing Sugar/Cocoa/Cornflour | 1 cup | 4½ oz | 120 g |
| Butter/Sugar | 2 tbsp | 1 oz | 25 g |
| (caster, granulated or brown, firmly packed) | ¼ cup | 2 oz | 50 g |
| | ½ cup | 4 oz | 100 g |
| | ¾ cup | 6 oz | 175 g |
| | 1 cup | 8 oz | 225 g |
| Liquids/Cream/Yogurt | ¼ cup | 2.5 fl oz | 60 ml |
| | ½ cup | 5 fl oz | 120 ml |
| | ¾ cup | 7.5 fl oz | 180 ml |
| | 1 cup | 10 fl oz | 240 ml |
| | 1 pt (2 cups) | 20 fl oz | 480 ml |
| Grated Cheese/Chopped Nuts | 1 cup | 4 oz | 100 g |
| Yeast | 1 cake, pkg | 4 oz fresh | 15 g |
| Rice | 1 cup | 8 oz | 230 g |

| Food Level | spoons to 1oz (25g) (approximate equivalents) |
|---|---|
| Flour, cornflour and other starch powders | 2 tablespoons |
| Fresh breadcrumbs and cake crumbs | 4 tablespoons |
| Rolled oats | 3 tablespoons |
| Rice | 2 tablespoons |
| Sugar | 2 tablespoons |
| Sultanas, seedless raisins, currants | 2 tablespoons |
| Butter | 2 tablespoons |
| Gelatine | 3 tablespoons |
| Syrup, treacle, honey | 1 tablespoon |

# Index

246

My most grateful thanks to the following special people
who have given me so much help and support:

My husband Oliver, Guy and Victoria, Edward, and Lucy and Mike. Also Tim Atkinson,
Kenny and Karen Flesh, Fenella Corr, Kath Davies, Wayne Davison, Steve Brand, and
all the team at Ballindalloch. So many thank yous as well to John Paul, Nick McCann,
Jamieson Eley, Simon Walton, Amy Davenport, David Clark, Patricia Lawson,
Alexandra Lawson, Andrea de Pree, Kate Pelham Burn, Sandra Macrae,
Kathy Mansfield, Robert Rattray, Andi Foxton, Joe Mckenzie, and the RSPB for their
photographs, and to Sue Leven for the delicious recipes.

Many apologies to anyone I have omitted; I have made every effort to contact all contributors, and copyright
holders of images and written content. If any omissions have occurred, I apologise, and amendments will be
incorporated in any subsequent editions.

Designed by Jamieson Eley

Published by Jarrold Publishing
Email: publications@jarrold-publishing.co.uk
www.jarrold-publishing.co.uk

Some people just can't help making a
difference in our lives.
By simply being who they are,
they make the world a little brighter,
a little warmer,
a little gentler,
and when they're gone we realise
how lucky we are to have known them.

## Gaelic Blessing

May the road rise to meet you
May the wind be always at your back
May the sun shine warm upon your face
And the rain fall soft upon your fields
And, until we meet again,
May God keep you in the hollow of His hand.